RETURN TO YOU

Discover The Power of The Enneagram To Unlock Your True Self and Embrace Personal Transformation

Simone Keys

Index

Introduction

Transforming power of the Enneagram

Welcome to a journey of self-discovery and personal growth. I am excited to introduce you to my new book: "Return to Yourself: Discover The Power of The Enneagram To Unlock Your True Self and Embrace Personal Transformation".

In these pages, I want us to discover the enigmatic world of the Enneagram and how it can help us to find the deepest secrets of our being.

The fast pace of modern life has filled us with permanent responsibilities, expectations and challenges. In the midst of this scenario, it is not difficult to lose our true self.

Often, we may find that we repeat patterns, face obstacles in our relationships, and feel disconnected from our true purpose.

This is where the Enneagram can help us. This ancient system for typifying personality is very accurate in describing our positive and negative characteristics, and the way we relate to other people.

The Enneagram shows us how our interaction with the environment and those around us are influenced by our unique characteristics.

In this book, I want to invite you to self-knowledge; we will identify our personality, to understand what motivates us and to overcome the challenges that stagnate us.

Here you will find tools and techniques with which you will be able to make significant changes in your life from the very first moment.

Through practical exercises, I will introduce you to each of the nine Enneagram personality types. Discover who you are, and how others see the world, understand their thoughts, emotions and actions from another perspective, a deeper and more compassionate one.

What you don't know about yourself can hurt you and your relationships; let me be your guide to understanding yourself, recognizing your strengths and weaknesses and overcoming the challenges you face.

At the end of this book, I give you four gifts, four special sections or bonuses, where I offer you visualization exercises, powerful affirmations and a couple of relevant topics to complement your experience with the Enneagram.

Get ready to embark on the road back to you, and you are about to begin an adventure that will improve your life forever.

With love,
Simone Keys

CHAPTER 1

What you don't know about yourself

In this first chapter, we will talk about the importance of knowing ourselves, and what it means not to do so, since not knowing how we are can harm us personally and affect our relationship with other people.

Without a clear understanding of our motivations, fears and desires, we can make poor decisions, perpetuate bad habits and distance ourselves from those we love. Ignorance about ourselves is an effect that prevents us from evolving.

It is important to know our own nature because each of us is unique, an unrepeatable combination of personality, talents and perspectives.

By knowing ourselves, we can align our actions and decisions with our values and objectives, so we can achieve great goals, gain greater satisfaction and enjoy well-being in every area of our lives.

Moreover, the connection between self-knowledge and spirituality is profound. When we embark on a journey of personal discovery, we open the door to a more intimate and authentic relationship with God.

The path to self-discovery is not always easy, but it is necessary for a fulfilling life. I am here to support you in this process, to share with you the wisdom of the Enneagram and to help you unveil the hidden truths within you.

So, get ready to discover the depth of your being; let's discover together your inner treasures. Let's open the door to authenticity and personal growth.

Let's go ahead and examine your repetitive patterns, which may manifest as self-criticism, fears or toxic relationships. You can start by identifying specific situations in which they manifest and reflect on how they arise.

Now, with respect to our subconscious beliefs, these have a great impact on how we perceive the world and how we behave.

They are often formed during our childhood and become ingrained in our being; in this case, I invite you to reflect on your beliefs and how they may be influencing your life today. What subconscious beliefs do you believe guide your choices and actions? Do they help you grow and prosper? Do they limit you and keep you stuck?

Sometimes, we are not aware of our strengths and abilities, but these are key to overcome the challenges we face and to achieve our goals.

Make a list of your talents, ask someone close to you to also list your positive qualities, compare the two and reflect on how you can leverage your strengths in different aspects of your life.

The process of discovering what you don't know about yourself is challenging but worth the effort, as you will have opportunities for transformation and improvement. Are you willing to step out of your comfort zone? What do you think you might discover by exploring your hidden facets?

Self-exploration is not linear or static, as you grow and evolve, new facets of you will emerge. I recommend you keep a journal, write down your emotions, thoughts, and discoveries; this will help you track your growth and identify recurring patterns.

The objective of this chapter is to help you identify the unknown aspects of yourself that may be harming you and your relationships. By facing them, you will be able to free yourself from limiting patterns, open yourself to new ways of being and relating to others.

This journey of self-discovery is unique to you, requiring patience, compassion and perseverance. Allow yourself to explore the unknown, challenge your ingrained beliefs and grow on your path to a more authentic and fulfilled version of yourself.

Let's start this journey of self-discovery together!

Why is self-knowledge important?

Self-knowledge is the foundation for personal growth, healthy relationships and our overall well-being. It is a revealing journey that allows us to understand our strengths, weaknesses, values, beliefs and motivations.

There are many important reasons why we should know ourselves, some of the most important of which are:

Self-acceptance, authenticity and congruence

By knowing our strengths, weaknesses, values and beliefs, we can accept ourselves as we are, be authentic, congruent with our values and desires, and enjoy more genuine and satisfying relationships with others.

Self-knowledge allows us to live according to our true values, rather than trying to fit into molds or satisfy external expectations. When we are aligned with our essence, we have greater inner coherence and integrity in all areas of our lives.

I give you the example of an employee whose values and passions are not aligned with the company where he works, even if he earns a lot of money and is successful, he will be dissatisfied and discouraged.

This person begins the process of self-knowledge and discovers that his true passion is to help others, so he decides to take another career path more related to his values. In this example, self-knowledge led this person to have a more authentic and meaningful life.

Conscious decision making

Self-knowledge gives us clarity to make conscious decisions based on our personal goals and needs.

By understanding our desires, priorities and limits, we make decisions according to our vision of life. Knowing ourselves allows us to control our life and direct it, without being influenced by others or falling into impulsive patterns.

Suppose someone is invited to participate in a project that requires a lot of time and effort. Without a good knowledge of himself, he might accept the offer without considering whether he has the ability or interest to carry it out.

Conversely, if you know your capabilities, you will assess whether the project aligns with your personal strengths, interests and goals and make an informed decision.

Improve interpersonal relationships

Self-knowledge allows us to establish healthy relationships. By understanding our emotions, needs and behavior patterns, we communicate better, set appropriate boundaries and cultivate relationships based on authenticity and mutual understanding.

We foster empathy and understanding in our relationships by understanding our own and others' tendencies.

Consider someone who has difficulty expressing his or her needs and emotions in a dating relationship. Through self-knowledge, this person can identify the reasons behind his or her difficulty in expression.

By understanding these internal dynamics, you will be able to improve your ability to communicate openly and assertively, and in turn, strengthen the relationship through honest and empathetic communication, fostering a deeper connection with your partner.

Personal development and growth

As we identify limiting patterns of behavior, we have the opportunity to discover areas for improvement, develop new skills, overcome internal obstacles and expand our potential.

Imagine someone who discovers his tendency to be very self-critical. Realizing this, he begins to practice self-compassion and tries to have a more positive mindset. Over time, he will have significant personal growth, increased confidence and emotional well-being.

Emotional and mental well-being

Self-knowledge allows us to recognize and manage emotions in a healthy way. By understanding our emotional reactions and their triggers, we can develop strategies to manage stress and promote our mental well-being, establishing self-care habits and seeking appropriate support if necessary.

Spiritual growth

By exploring our own essence and connecting with our spirituality, we can find greater meaning, purpose and significance in our lives.

Self-knowledge and relationships

It is surprising how a lack of self-knowledge harms us by hindering our ability to establish relationships.

During the process of self-awareness, we will see how our unconscious actions, unmanaged emotions and negative behavioral patterns can affect ourselves and those around us.

For now, these are some of the ways in which not knowing ourselves can harm us and affect our relationships:

Repetition of harmful patterns

Self-knowledge favors that we repeat negative behavior patterns without being aware of it. We fall into toxic dynamics when we overreact to certain situations, or when we act impulsively without understanding the cause of our actions.

Without understanding our ingrained beliefs, wounds and behaviors, we are likely to repeat harmful patterns in our relationships, becoming trapped in a cycle of endless conflict.

Imagine someone who has grown up in an aggressive and conflictive environment. If he doesn't know himself, he may inadvertently adopt that same form of communication in his relationships, generating a pattern of constant arguments and misunderstandings, which will damage the quality of his relationships and hinder his emotional connection.

Lack of self-acceptance and self-esteem

Lack of self-knowledge can lead to a lack of acceptance and self-esteem. If we do not understand our strengths, qualities and values, we are more likely to compare ourselves with others and feel inadequate, which lowers our self-esteem and leads us to constantly seek external validation.

A person who does not know themselves may spend most of their time trying to fit in with what others expect of them; instead of recognizing their own wants and needs, they strive to please others; this can lead to resentment, frustration, as well as superficial and inauthentic relationships.

Difficulties in communication and empathy

Ignorance of our own emotions and needs hinders our effective communication and understanding of others.

By not understanding our own emotions and motivations, it is difficult to empathize with the experiences and feelings of others; we are quick to judge people without understanding their perspective or ignoring the emotional needs of those around us, causing tension in our relationships.

When we do not know ourselves, it is more difficult to communicate our needs, desires and emotions clearly and effectively. We struggle to express what we really want or need, and this can lead to misunderstandings and conflicts in our relationships.

Suppose someone is unaware that he or she is repressing his or her emotions. In a relationship, this confuses and generates misunderstandings, since this lack of emotional expression can be interpreted as indifference or disinterest, hindering the emotional connection and the building of a relationship based on trust and empathy.

Unbalanced relationships

Lack of self-knowledge can lead us to unbalanced relationships, where we fail to set healthy boundaries, allow others to take advantage of our vulnerabilities, create emotional dependency or constantly sacrifice ourselves for the well-being of others to the neglect of our own.

Self-boycott and personal stagnation

Not knowing ourselves can lead us to self-blame, denying our abilities and impeding our personal growth. We limit ourselves by not recognizing our potential and missing opportunities.

Now that we are aware of how self-doubt hurts us and can affect our relationships, it is time to take action. Here are some practical strategies that can be very useful in getting to know ourselves:

Self-reflection

Self-reflection will help you go deeper inside yourself and better understand who you really are.

Take time to ask yourself how you feel, what motivates you, what your values are, and what patterns of behavior you have observed in yourself.

Seeking feedback

Constructive feedback from others can give valuable insight and help you discover aspects of yourself that you may not have considered. Seek the opinions of people you are close to and trust. Ask them how they perceive you, what strengths they see in you and in what areas they think you could improve.

The practice of self-compassion

We all have strengths and weaknesses, but personal growth involves accepting and loving every part of ourselves. Be self-compassionate, accept yourself unconditionally, forgive yourself for your mistakes, be kind to yourself and don't judge yourself harshly.

Exploration of self-knowledge techniques

Techniques such as meditation, yoga, therapy or the use of tools such as the Enneagram will help you understand your thought patterns, emotions and behaviors.

Breaking patterns that stagnate

It is possible that at some point, we have felt trapped in repetitive cycles, trying to move towards our goals and dreams, but without success.

These repetitive patterns can manifest in our interpersonal relationships, career, health or spiritual development, impeding our personal growth and keeping us from the life we desire.

We have the power to break these cycles and free ourselves from stagnation. To do so, we need to recognize that these patterns are the product of ingrained beliefs, fears and automatic behaviors.

Review your own history and identify the patterns that stagnate you; this is the first step to transform them into opportunities for growth and improvement.

In order to break the patterns that stagnate us, it is necessary to recognize them and become aware of them. This is achieved by identifying, with mindfulness, the repetitive behaviors, thoughts and beliefs that limit us.

Likewise, it is necessary to recognize how they emerge in our lives. What recurring patterns have you observed in your life? How are they limiting you? What fosters these patterns in your life?

Self-awareness allows us to recognize when we are trapped in a negative pattern. These can manifest in various ways, some of which are:

Limiting thoughts: Negative, self-critical, limiting thoughts can become ingrained patterns that keep us stuck, keep us from seeing our true potential, keep us from pursuing our true passion, tell us that we are not good enough, that we don't deserve to succeed or that we won't overcome certain obstacles.

Self-defeating behaviors: Procrastination, indiscipline or avoiding responsibilities, are behaviors that can become negative patterns and stagnate us, prevent us from taking action, reaching our full potential and achieving our goals.

Comfort zone: Resistance to change and attachment to comfort can become a negative pattern that keeps us in a monotonous life without growth. Staying within our comfort zone prevents us from exploring new experiences, facing challenges and discovering our true potential.

We've already identified some negative patterns that are holding us back, but how do we get rid of them? Here are some practical strategies that can help us:

Take deliberate action: Identify what you can do to change your situation and start taking the first steps, even if you are uncomfortable or fearful. Real change only happens when we commit, take action, and challenge our comfort zone.

For example, if your pattern is procrastination, set daily or weekly goals and make a commitment to meet them without delay, create a detailed action plan, set reminders and seek support to maintain your motivation. This exercise will help you stop procrastinating and establish new productive habits.

Question limiting beliefs: Question ingrained beliefs; they often support negative patterns, instead we can replace them with positive, empowering thoughts.

Cultivate a growth mindset: We must be willing to step out of our comfort zone, take risks and face our fears to overcome stagnation. Breaking limiting patterns requires adopting a growth mindset, in which we see opportunities for learning and growth in challenges.

Set goals and concrete actions: Setting realistic objectives and designing a detailed action plan to make the necessary transformations in our lives can help us break patterns and free ourselves from the cycle of stagnation.

Seek support and guidance: We are not alone in trying to break limiting patterns, we can seek professional help and guidance from mentors or loved ones; this is very valuable as it gives us new perspectives, motivation and the necessary support to overcome challenges.

Through dedication and commitment to our personal growth, we can free ourselves from the patterns that keep us stuck; this process of change does not happen overnight; it takes time, patience and self-compassion.

Every small step you take in the direction of change is valuable; celebrate your accomplishments, no matter how small, and they will keep you motivated and confident in yourself and your progress towards personal transformation.

Be self-compassionate, accept yourself as you are throughout this process, recognize that breaking patterns is a challenge and that you may encounter obstacles in the process. Allow yourself to make mistakes, learn from them and move forward.

You have the power to break the patterns that keep you stuck. By challenging your limiting thoughts, adopting new behaviors and stepping out of your comfort zone, you will be opening the path to personal growth and fulfillment.

You are the protagonist of your own story, move towards a more satisfying life. Change begins now!

Spirituality and self-knowledge

For centuries, many spiritual traditions have recognized that the path to growth involves a deep understanding of our own nature. Self-knowledge and spirituality are intertwined at their very base, the inner quest, and through it, both can guide us toward a more meaningful life.

With introspection, reflection and observation of our mind and emotions, we can discover our true essence. This process allows us to connect with something deeper and transcendental beyond our own existence.

Imagine that a person has experienced a lack of purpose in your life, feels a void in his or her being, and instead of looking outside for answers, prefers to meditate, practice reflective writing or maintain contact with nature to try to get into his or her own being.

Thus he begins to delve deeper within, discovering his values, passions and a sense of connection to something greater than himself. This inner search is a catalyst for awakening spirituality and finding greater meaning in his life.

As we get to know ourselves better, we begin to develop a greater understanding of our needs, desires and life purpose. This self-exploration allows us to align ourselves with our true nature, helps us shed masks and roles we wear to fit into society.

By accepting your inner voice and making choices in accordance with your authenticity, you can experience a deeper connection with yourself and a sense of spiritual fulfillment.

Spiritual practices allow us to explore our minds, emotions and relationships with others, through meditation, prayer, the study of sacred texts and participation in spiritual communities; with these practices we can cultivate full consciousness and connection with something greater than ourselves.

Between spirituality and self-knowledge, there is a deep and meaningful connection. By connecting with your spirituality, you discover an inner source of strength and wisdom that guides you in your process of self-knowledge and as we self-discover ourselves, we find our spiritual essence.

A practical exercise to deepen this connection is to dedicate time to contemplation and introspection. Set aside a few minutes upon waking or before going to sleep, reflect on your thoughts, emotions and experiences of the day. Notice how you feel in each moment and how your actions align with your values.

A deeper understanding of yourself and your spiritual connection will open doors to a fuller, more meaningful and authentic life.

CHAPTER 2

Discovering the true self

In this chapter, we are going to dive into the world of the Enneagram, an ancient system for typifying the personality that allows us to know ourselves and others in a deeper way.

Through this powerful approach, we will discover how the nine personality types described by the Enneagram can reveal hidden aspects of the way we are and how we can use this knowledge to live a more fulfilling and authentic life.

I particularly think that the Enneagram is much more than a simple classification of personalities; for me, it is a powerful tool which invites us to explore how complex and deep our own psychology can be.

Each of the nine personality types of the Enneagram represents a unique pattern of thoughts, emotions and behaviors.

As we explore these personality types, strengthen our processes of self-exploration and self-discovery, we can understand our motivations, fears and behavioral patterns, free ourselves from the limitations that hold us back and achieve significant personal growth.

The Enneagram also allows us to be more compassionate, empathetic and understanding towards others, promotes more effective communication and improves our relationships because it allows us to see the world through different eyes and understand how the motivations and actions of others are influenced by their personality type.

The Enneagram is a tool that allows us to break limiting patterns, freeing us from ingrained beliefs and negative behaviors. It is a compass that guides us towards our true self, allowing us to live in coherence with our authenticity and maximum potential.

To begin exploring the Enneagram, it is advisable to take a questionnaire or test and identify your personality type, then research and understand the characteristics, motivations and challenges associated with your specific type.

Reflect on how these characteristics manifest in your daily life, and how you might use this information to further your personal growth.

As you deepen your understanding of the different types and how they relate to you, you will be better prepared to face life's challenges, improve your relationships and increase your own self-awareness.

History and origin of the Enneagram

The Enneagram has been used for centuries to understand the different dimensions of human nature. It has its origins in ancient spiritual and philosophical traditions, believed to date back more than 4,000 years, in the mystical teachings of the Middle East and ancient esoteric traditions.

It was in the 1960s when the Enneagram began to gain popularity in the West, thanks to figures such as Oscar Ichazo and Claudio Naranjo.

Ichazo, a Bolivian mystic, introduced the concept of the nine personality types and established the basis for their study and understanding.

Later, Naranjo, a Chilean psychiatrist and psychologist, merged Ichazo's teachings with modern psychology, giving this system a more contemporary perspective.

Through its nine distinct personality types, the Enneagram provides us with a roadmap to explore our inner motivations, fears and strengths.

Each type has its unique strengths and challenges, and by exploring them, we can get to know ourselves more deeply and discover areas for personal growth.

To better understand these personality types, it is useful to look at examples from everyday life in which the behavior in a given situation is described.

I invite you to read the following sentences and, when you finish reading the book, go back and identify which personality type you consider corresponds to each of them (you can write down the number of each type next to each sentence):

( ) This personality type has a deep sensitivity and creativity, seeks to express itself in a unique way through art or personal authenticity.

( ) This personality type may obsess over the smallest details of their work, to make sure everything is flawless before presenting it to others.

( ) This personality type has an innate ability to promote harmony and avoid conflict, seeking peace and stability in their relationships.

( ) This personality type devotes a great deal of time and energy to caring for others, even sacrificing their own needs in the process.

( ) This personality type can spend hours immersed in research and study of topics of interest to them, seeking knowledge and deep understanding.

( ) This personality type constantly strives for success in his or her career, placing emphasis on his or her image and external achievements.

( ) This personality type has a strong need for security, seeks approval and guidance from others in decision-making.

( ) This type of personality constantly seeks new experiences and emotions, preventing boredom and routine.

( ) This personality type assumes leadership and authority in different situations, defending the weakest and fighting for justice.

The Enneagram is a powerful tool to discover our essence and better understand others. It does not seek to pigeonhole or limit us into a category, it guides us to understand our tendencies and motivations, recognize negative patterns, and break self-imposed limitations in order to reach our full potential.

As we deepen our understanding of the 9 personality types, we unlock the potential to cultivate more authentic relationships, nurture our spiritual growth and live a fuller, more meaningful life.

The 9 personality types of the Enneagram

When we explore our tendencies and patterns, the Enneagram is a valuable guide to discover our true self and understand the complexities of our personality, with it, we can work on our personal growth and develop healthier and more meaningful relationships.

According to the Enneagram, each individual falls into one of nine personality types, which describe how we perceive and relate to the world, as well as their unique strengths and challenges.

These are the 9 personality types of the Enneagram:

- Type one: The Perfectionist
- Type two: The Helper
- Type three: The Triumphant
- Type four: The Individualist
- Type five: The Observer
- Type six: The Loyal
- Type seven: The Enthusiast
- Type eight: The Challenger
- Type nine: The Peacemaker

In the following section, I will briefly describe them and, subsequently, I will dedicate a complete chapter to each one of them, with valuable information that will surely be very useful to you.

During the reading, I recommend you to practice the following exercise:

- Observe how the different types interact in your environment, whether in your family, friends, co-workers or any other significant relationship.
- Try to understand their perspectives and motivations, which can help foster more effective communication and harmony in your interactions.
- Don't limit yourself to a single interpretation of your personality type; explore your gray areas, discover new facets of yourself and use this information as a starting point for your personal growth.
- Work on the areas you want to improve and cultivate the strengths that define you.

Through this journey of self-exploration, we can unlock our potential, overcome obstacles and achieve greater harmony and authenticity in our lives.

Characteristics of the 9 personality types

As I mentioned earlier, each personality type has unique characteristics that influence the way we perceive the world, relate to others and face life's challenges.

Here are the 9 personality types according to the Enneagram:

Type one: The Perfectionist

Type 1 people are diligent, disciplined and strive to do things correctly, are improvement-oriented, and are characterized by a strong sense of duty and a quest for perfection.

On the other hand, they can become excessively self-demanding, very critical of themselves and also of others.

A Type 1 person may have very high standards for their work and strive to correct every little detail in pursuit of perfection; they may also feel uncomfortable if they perceive that there is disorder or lack of organization in their environment, and will strive to establish order to maintain harmony.

Type two: The Helper

Type 2 people are generous, caring, helpful and other-oriented, they are empathetic and constantly looking for ways to provide support and love to those around them. They have a great need to be needed and loved, and are often dedicated to helping and caring for others.

On the other hand, they may have difficulty setting boundaries and prioritizing their own needs, arguably neglecting their own needs in favor of satisfying those of others.

A type 2 person may feel happy and fulfilled by helping a friend in a time of need, even if it means neglecting his or her own well-being.

Type three: El Triunfador

Type 3 people are ambitious, success-oriented and highly motivated, seek approval and recognition from others, and tend to measure their worth by their accomplishments and outward appearance. They are highly competitive and strive to excel in everything they do.

On the other hand, they may have difficulty connecting with their deepest emotions and pay too much attention to image and outward appearance.

A Type 3 person may devote a lot of time and energy to building an image of success in their professional life, but may neglect other important areas, such as personal relationships, their own health, or struggle to find time for relaxation activities and personal enjoyment.

Type four: The Individualist

Type 4 people are creative, sensitive, value authenticity, tend to be emotionally deep, also seek a special, unique and meaningful identity and emotional connection in their relationships.

On the other hand, they often experience intense emotions, emotional ups and downs and may be prone to melancholy.

A Type 4 person may spend time exploring their creativity through art, music or writing to express their inner uniqueness, may find beauty and meaning in a work of art, a melody or an emotionally intense moment, but may also feel misunderstood or excluded because of their high emotional sensitivity.

Type five: The Observer

Type 5 people are reflective, observant, curious, independent, have an unquenchable thirst for knowledge, are introverted, prefer solitude to explore and reflect on the world around them. They have an analytical mind and enjoy research and learning.

On the other hand, they may have difficulty sharing their knowledge and emotions with others.

A Type 5 person may be comfortable and satisfied with immersing themselves in a book or doing in-depth research on a topic of interest, but may find it challenging to express their thoughts and emotions in social situations.

Type six: The Loyal

Type 6 people are loyal, responsible and security-conscious, seeking certainty and stability in their lives, and tend to anticipate possible dangers.

On the other hand, they may experience anxiety and self-doubt, so they seek the protection and support of others.

A Type 6 individual may have a cautious approach to important decisions, carefully assessing risks and seeking input from others.

Type seven: The Enthusiast

Type 7 people are optimistic, adventurous, like to explore different options, constantly looking for new experiences and positive emotions to avoid boredom or routine.

On the other hand, they may have difficulty coping with negative emotions and seek distractions to avoid pain or discomfort.

A Type 7 person may be excited and enthusiastic about planning a trip or a new activity, but may have difficulty coping with difficult or boring difficulties.

Type eight: The Challenger

Type 8 people are strong, direct, have a great need for control and autonomy, are natural leaders, and defend their beliefs and values with determination.

On the other hand, they may have difficulty showing vulnerability and trusting others.

A Type 8 person can take on leadership roles and make bold decisions with confidence, but may also experience challenges in emotional openness and delegating responsibility.

Type nine: The Peacemaker

Type 9 people are peaceful, conciliatory, seek harmony and tranquility in their relationships, tend to avoid conflict and may sacrifice their own needs to maintain peace.

On the other hand, they may have difficulty expressing their opinions and asserting their individuality.

A Type 9 individual may feel comfortable and happy being in a peaceful and harmonious environment, but may have difficulty defending his or her own needs and desires in a conflict situation.

Exercises to identify personality types

Identifying your personality type is essential for self-discovery and personal growth. When you understand your behavior patterns and the way you relate to the world, you can build on your strengths and work on the areas that need development.

It also allows you to understand your emotional reactions, your recurring challenges and ways in which you can improve your relationships with others.

To this effect, I propose you to perform three exercises that will allow you to deepen your self-knowledge and better understand your thought patterns, behavior and underlying motivations.

Let's start with the first of the three exercises:

Exercise 1: The Enneagram Questionnaire

This brief questionnaire is designed to identify your possible personality type according to the Enneagram system.

It consists of 10 short statements that you will rate on a scale from 0 to 5, according to what best represents your behavior, motivations or preferences. Do not worry, there are no right or wrong answers.

The objective is to get a clearer picture of your tendencies and preferences in different aspects of your life. By answering honestly, you will be able to get a clearer picture of your dominant personality type.

Instructions:

- Carefully read each sentence of the questionnaire
- Select the option that best represents you
- Rate your answer by assigning the score that you consider most appropriate, according to this scale:

  0 - Not applicable or not sure

  1 - I do not identify myself

  2 - I do not identify myself to a great extent

  3 - I somewhat identify myself

  4 - I identify myself to a great extent

  5 - I totally identify myself
- At the end, add up your scores and you will be able to determine which Enneagram personality type you are most likely to have

Questionnaire:

1. I like to be in the spotlight and be praised.
2. I prefer to be alone than to socialize in large groups.

3. I strive to maintain peace and avoid conflict
4. I tend to analyze and reflect a lot on things.
5. I find it easy to connect emotionally with others
6. I like to have a routine and structure in my life.
7. I am always looking for new experiences and adventures
8. I value independence and personal autonomy
9. I am very attentive to detail and a perfectionist.
10. I care about the welfare and needs of others

Results:

Find your personality type according to your total score:

type one: Total score between 20 and 30

type two: Total score between 31 and 40

type three: Total score between 41 and 50

type four: Total score between 51 and 60

type five: Total score between 61 and 70

type six: Total score between 71 and 80

type seven: Total score between 81 and 90

type eight: Total score between 91 and 100

type nine: Total score between 101 and 110

This questionnaire is only an initial guide to explore your personality type in the Enneagram system, this is a complex system that requires deeper analysis and understanding to accurately identify your personality type.

The Enneagram does not define who you are, it only provides a greater understanding of your behavioral patterns, it offers the opportunity to grow and develop.

To gain a more accurate and deeper understanding, I recommend reading more about each of the personality types and their main characteristics, as well as seeking advice from professionals trained in the Enneagram.

The Enneagram recognizes that each individual is unique and may have traits and characteristics of various types. Take this information as a guide to know yourself better and to understand how your thought patterns, emotions and behavior can potentially influence your life and relationships.

Exercise 2: Reflection and self-observation

In addition to the questionnaire, I invite you to reflect on your daily life and carry out a process of self-observation.

Take time to analyze your reactions, emotions and behaviors in various situations, observe how you relate to others, how you handle stress and how you deal with challenges.

You can keep a personal journal where you record your observations and reflections. For example, you could write down how you feel and how you react when you are under pressure at work, in a family discussion or in a creative project.

These observations will develop valuable clues about your predominant personality type.

Exercise 3: Searching for patterns and trends

Another useful approach to identifying your personality type is to look for patterns and trends in your life. See if there are recurring behaviors, distinguishing characteristics or common themes in your experiences.

Ask yourself: Are there situations in which I tend to stand out or feel more comfortable? What aspects of my personality are consistent over time and in different contexts?

For example, if you notice that you tend to be a perfectionist in all areas of your life, it is possible that your personality type is related to perfectionism and the desire to do things flawlessly. If you find that you enjoy planning and organization in all your projects, it is likely that your personality type is associated with structure and efficiency.

Remember that these exercises and reflections are only tools to help you in the process of identifying your personality type. The objective is not to pigeonhole you into a category, but to understand the main characteristics of your personality type and use that knowledge as a tool for your personal growth.

By identifying your personality type, you will be able to develop greater understanding and empathy for yourself, as well as improve your interpersonal relationships and your authenticity in the world.

CHAPTER 3

Personality type 1: The Perfectionist

In the development of this chapter, we will discover and analyze the Enneagram type one personality, together we will discover the different facets of "The Perfectionist", its main characteristics, motivations, influence, what aspects they should improve and how they can do it.

To begin with, type one's tend to be highly self-demanding; they tend to have very high standards for themselves and others, constantly seeking perfection in every area of their lives.

However, being overly critical of oneself and others can lead the Perfectionist to feel dissatisfied with him/herself.

To improve this condition, Perfectionists could work on self-compassion, which can be a powerful tool for type ones, as it allows them to balance the permanent search for perfection with self-acceptance and self-love.

When type ones learn to treat each other with kindness and understanding, they are freed from self-recrimination and enjoy greater inner peace.

Type one personality

The type one personality is characterized by having a strong sense of duty and being highly self-demanding. Their standards of action are high both for themselves and others.

They seek constant improvement and are always willing to correct any imperfections they perceive. Because of their constant search for perfection, they tend to be critical of others and excessively self-critical of themselves.

They have solid principles, ethics and values, as well as a strong connection to a sense of what is right. They are responsible and reliable, fulfill their commitments and responsibilities.

They are detail-oriented and meticulous, can perceive mistakes quickly and have a strong need to correct them. They are also disciplined and organized, so they prefer rigorously to structure their time and environment rather than act without a plan.

They may be seen as controlling because of their desire to maintain order and excellence in all areas of their lives.

They are motivated by a strong desire to improve and do things right, they aspire to perfection in all areas of their lives, so they are constantly striving for excellence and quality in everything they do.

The Perfectionist is also motivated to improve everything, both personally and in their environment. They want to be the best version of themselves, so they strive for a high level of competence and achievement in their activities.

Doing things correctly is one of their greatest motivations. They seek precision, accuracy and consistency in their actions, always with the goal of meeting the highest standards.

Perfection is a constant goal for perfectionists; although it is difficult to achieve, their motivation comes from firmly believing that, by pursuing perfection, they can achieve an exceptional level of quality and excellence in all areas of their life.

The type one personality is characterized by seeking justice and fairness in all areas of life. These people strive to live according to their principles and values, and expect the same from others. When things do not meet their expectations, they may experience frustration and seek ways to correct the situation.

Type Ones feel the need to have control over situations to make sure they are carried out correctly. They are meticulous about details and strive to do things the right way, following a precise plan.

They feel a responsibility to correct mistakes and contribute to the welfare of others, as their sense of duty and work ethic drive them to strive for perfectionism and excellence in everything they do.

With respect to the impact of their personality on their different aspects of life, Perfectionists can be very detail-oriented and work with precision in the work environment. They are very good at roles that require close attention and following rules.

In their interpersonal relationships, they can be critical and have high expectations, so they are often perceived as rigid or inflexible, which can generate tensions in close relationships.

In terms of self-care, Type Ones can be very disciplined and mindful of their well-being. They may have structured exercise and healthy eating routines.

Interaction with the world and relationships

The high standards Perfectionists tend to have with themselves and others influence their relationships and their interaction with the world around them.

Let's analyze the influence of perfectionism on their interpersonal relationships, their sense of social responsibility and their ability to adapt to different situations.

Interpersonal relationships

Type Ones seek excellence in everything they do, including their personal relationships. By being so critical of themselves and others, they are likely to generate tension and conflict.

For example, when a Perfectionist is inflexible and does not accept his or her partner's mistakes, it can lead to a rigid relationship.

For one, it is advisable to learn to be more compassionate and tolerant, to become more flexible in their search for perfection and to understand that we can all make mistakes.

Sense of social responsibility

Perfectionists have a strong sense of duty and what is right; they may feel responsible for correcting injustices and improving their environment.

This can be manifested when participating in social organizations, when defending just causes and with their commitment to comply with norms and rules.

However, it is also important that they learn to balance their sense of responsibility with the acceptance that they cannot change or control everything.

Adaptability

Perfectionists may have difficulty adapting to change and unforeseen situations; they are uncomfortable with uncertainty.

They may experience anxiety when faced with a sudden change in their daily routine or a project that does not go according to plan.

It is important that they learn to be more flexible, to accept that the world is imperfect and that things do not always go as expected, to balance their desire for perfection with acceptance of imperfections, and to practice compassion for themselves and others.

Overcoming the need for perfection

The need for perfection can negatively impact some aspects of the Perfectionist's life. While striving for excellence is a valuable quality, this is a hindrance if it becomes a constant demand that generates permanent dissatisfaction.

People can experience high levels of stress and anxiety when unattainable standards are imposed, or when they are harshly criticized for any failure or mistake, which is emotionally and physically draining, and detracts from their overall well-being.

Overcoming the need for perfection requires acceptance of self and circumstances. It is important that the type one recognizes that absolute perfection does not exist and that mistakes are part of the human experience.

To improve this aspect, they can be more understanding and kind to themselves when they make mistakes or face challenges. For example, they can remember that making mistakes is an opportunity for learning and growth rather than seeing it as a personal failure.

Perfectionists tend to set unattainable and demanding goals; in this case, it is important that they learn to set realistic and flexible goals, considering their own capabilities and limitations.

In this case, they can try to break down large goals into smaller tasks, and celebrate achievement with each step taken rather than upon reaching total perfection. This will allow them to experience satisfaction and greater motivation to move forward without frustration.

Self-care is essential for the Perfectionist to manage their need for perfection. A good start is to dedicate time to relaxing and pleasurable activities, such as exercising, reading, hobbies, or enjoying nature; these activities will help them balance their focus on achievement and nurture their emotional and physical well-being.

Overcoming the need for perfection is a gradual process, where the ultimate goal is to develop a more compassionate and flexible mindset, accepting one's own and others' strengths and limitations.

Overcoming the need for perfection is an important step toward self-compassion and emotional well-being. Through acceptance, realistic goal setting and self-care, Type Ones can free themselves from perfectionism and thus, move forward in their personal growth process, enjoy healthier relationships and a more fulfilling and satisfying life.

Cultivating self-compassion

Perfectionists tend to be self-demanding and critical of themselves; their constant pursuit of excellence can lead to overwhelming pressure and a constant feeling of dissatisfaction.

For them, self-compassion is fundamental, accepting themselves with kindness, compassion, recognizing their humanity, allowing mistakes and failures without judging themselves implacably, and thus, developing a healthy, more balanced personality and advancing towards their personal growth.

An effective way to cultivate self-compassion is to practice *mindfulness*, to be aware and live in the present moment without judgment.

Perfectionists can benefit from applying mindfulness to their critical and self-critical thoughts, observing them without identifying with them, replacing them with more compassionate and kind thoughts. For example, instead of saying to themselves, "I always do everything wrong", they can change it to "I am human, I make mistakes and that's okay".

Treating yourself with kindness and care involves prioritizing self-care and self-reflection without judging yourself negatively. Setting healthy boundaries is another essential aspect, learning to say "no" when necessary will prevent overload and burnout.

Self-compassion allows us to grow from self-love and accept our being instead of being self-demanding and merciless critics. This does not mean settling for mediocrity; on the contrary, it implies recognizing our limitations and defects, as well as our intrinsic value as human beings.

Cultivating self-compassion requires practice and patience, and can be a challenging process for those who have become accustomed to being critical of themselves. However, the benefits are enormous; it allows us to be more compassionate and understanding, strengthens emotional resilience and improves overall quality of life.

To cultivate self-compassion, we can perform some practical exercises that will help us develop a healthier relationship with ourselves and overcome the need for perfection:

Practice self-reflection: Reflect on your self-critical thoughts and how they arise. Notice when you judge yourself harshly and challenge those thoughts, ask yourself if they really benefit you or if you can adopt a more compassionate perspective.

Write a letter of self-compassion: Write a letter in which you address yourself with kindness and compassion. Acknowledge your efforts, accept your imperfections, and give yourself words of encouragement and support.

Practice self-care: Make a list of activities that give you pleasure and relaxation, and commit to doing at least one of them every day. It could be reading a book, enjoying a relaxing bath, taking a walk outdoors, or taking a moment to breathe deeply and relax.

Accept mistakes as opportunities for growth: Instead of punishing yourself for failing, face the situation as a learning opportunity. Recognize that we can all make mistakes, it is part of our growth process. Allow yourself to learn from them and move on.

Self-compassion is a personal journey unique to each individual. There is no magic formula, but with practice and patience, you can develop greater self-love and acceptance of yourself.

Assessment: By practicing self-compassion, Perfectionists can have greater inner peace, enjoy their intrinsic worth, live with greater joy and authenticity, have a healthy relationship with themselves, and improve their interpersonal relationships with understanding and empathy.

CHAPTER 4

Personality type 2: The Helper

"The Helper" or individuals with Enneagram personality type two, have a strong desire to be loved and appreciated. Furthermore, they tend to be actively involved in the lives of others, generously offering their help and support.

They are caring, empathetic and helpful people, enjoy being helpful and strive to create deep emotional connections with others.

They focus primarily on the needs of others, and may feel uncomfortable if they receive help or attention for themselves.

In their eagerness to satisfy the needs of others, they may neglect their own needs and set unhealthy boundaries, which leads to feeling overburdened, resentful, as well as physically and emotionally exhausted.

Type two personality

Type twos are altruistic in nature, generous, empathetic and always willing to help others; they are known for their ability to provide emotional support.

They are extremely perceptive, highly attuned to the emotional needs of others and feel fulfilled when they make a difference in someone else's life.

They tend to establish warm and close relationships, enjoy deep emotional connection. They are excellent listeners, their generosity and willingness to help often make them well-liked and appreciated in their social environment.

Helpers have a compassionate personality. It is common to see them giving support to a friend in difficult times, volunteering their time and energy to help a loved one, or devoting their free time to volunteer for a charity.

One of their main motivations is the desire to earn the affection and attention of others in order to feel loved and valued.

However, they may fall into the pattern of over-giving and neglect their own needs in the process, so it is important that they balance their desire to help others with caring for themselves.

They may sometimes face challenges in setting healthy boundaries, may have difficulty saying "no" or getting help themselves, as their self-esteem is often tied to the attention and appreciation of others.

They may also feel guilty if they are not permanently available to help, and they may resent it if they feel that their collaboration is not recognized or is undervalued.

It is important for Helpers to reflect on their motivation for helping. Do they do it for external recognition and approval or because they genuinely want to genuinely help others?

Taking the time to explore their motivations will allow them to better understand their behavioral pattern and make adjustments to move forward in their personal growth process.

As Helpers become aware of their tendency to sacrifice their needs, they can begin to set healthy boundaries that allow them to take care of themselves while still providing support to others.

With self-compassion and unconditional love for themselves, type twos can avoid burnout and build more balanced and satisfying relationships.

As they develop greater awareness of themselves and their needs, they will be able to communicate more effectively, clearly expressing their needs and desires in an assertive manner without feeling guilty about taking care of themselves.

This will also provide them with the opportunity to receive support and help when they need it, which is essential to maintain their emotional balance and establish more authentic, meaningful and satisfying relationships.

Strengths and weaknesses in relationships

The innate desire to support others can have a significant impact on the personal relationships of The Helpers, which also means facing challenges.

Let's discover how the characteristics of type twos can influence relationship dynamics, how they might leverage their strengths and address their weaknesses to have healthier, more balanced relationships.

Some of the valuable strengths of The Helpers in relating to others include:

Generosity and empathy: They are highly empathetic and have a natural ability to understand the needs and emotions of others. This ability allows them to provide genuine support and be there for their loved ones in times of difficulty.

Care and Attention: They care deeply about the well-being of others and are willing to make sacrifices to ensure that they are comfortable and happy. Their ability to pay attention to detail and offer practical help is appreciated by those around them.

Emotional connection: They value intimate relationships and are willing to open up emotionally. Their ability to establish deep and sincere bonds creates an atmosphere of trust and closeness in relationships.

Ability to resolve conflicts: They are excellent mediators and seek harmony in relationships. They have an innate ability to identify the needs of both parties and find win-win solutions.

While Helpers have many strengths in relationships, they also face some weaknesses and challenges:

Excessive sacrifice of one's own needs: They tend to put the needs of others above their own, often neglecting their own self-care. This can lead to emotional and physical exhaustion, as well as emotional dependence on external validation and approval.

Feeling of being indispensable: They may have an intense need to be needed by others, which can lead to overcommitment and difficulty setting healthy boundaries in relationships. This can lead to long-term resentment and burnout.

Seeking external validation: They may depend on the approval and recognition of others. Their sense of self-worth may be tied to how much they can help others, which can result in a lack of self-esteem and difficulty setting personal boundaries.

Difficulty receiving help: Despite their helpful nature, Helpers may have difficulty accepting help offered by others. They may be uncomfortable being on the receiving end and resist showing vulnerability. This creates imbalances in their relationships, as they may give a lot, but find it very difficult to receive.

Some actions that can help Helpers overcome their weaknesses and cultivate healthy relationships are:

Self-awareness and self-care: Helpers can benefit from developing greater awareness of their own needs and prioritizing self-care. Learning to set healthy boundaries and taking time to meet their own needs will help them avoid burnout and maintain balance in their relationships.

Open and honest communication: It is critical for Helpers to learn to communicate their own needs and desires in relationships. Expressing their feelings and expectations in a clear and respectful manner will help them establish open communication and avoid built-up resentment.

Cultivate self-compassion: Self-compassion allows Helpers to recognize their own needs and seek their well-being without feeling guilty. They can be more self-compassionate by setting healthy boundaries, recognizing and meeting their own needs.

Learning to receive help: Recognizing the importance of receiving support from others is essential for The Helpers. Learning to accept help openly and gratefully will strengthen their relationships and remind them that they also deserve to be cared for and supported.

Setting healthy boundaries

Helpers are generous and empathetic people who have a strong drive to care for and support others. However, they may face difficulties in setting clear boundaries and balancing their own needs.

Type twos often have difficulty saying "no" and setting clear boundaries because they fear hurting or disappointing others. However, it is important to understand that setting healthy boundaries is a form of self-care and contributes to more balanced and authentic relationships.

Boundaries help maintain personal autonomy, prevent burnout and foster relationships based on mutual respect.

Helpers need to watch for signs that their boundaries are blurred or being violated. This can manifest itself in feeling exhausted, resentful, or overwhelmed by the demands of others.

Recognizing these signs will allow them to take action to set healthy boundaries and protect their well-being, both physically and emotionally.

Saying "no" can be challenging for them, as their compassionate nature drives them to say "yes" even when they don't want to.

Learning assertive communication techniques and expressing boundaries clearly and respectfully will help them set limits without feeling guilty or negatively affecting their relationships. They can practice phrases such as: "I appreciate your trust in me, but I cannot commit to helping you at this time.

Setting healthy boundaries involves recognizing and prioritizing their own needs and well-being. This may include setting aside time for activities that bring them joy and rest, establishing self-care routines, and learning to delegate tasks to others.

They may also seek support from friends, family or mental health professionals. By talking about their challenges and emotions, they can gain clarity and gain outside perspectives to help them make decisions that are more balanced and consistent with their needs.

It is important to keep in mind that setting healthy boundaries does not mean giving up helping others, but rather finding a balance that allows them to take care of themselves at the same time. In doing so, Helpers will be able to play their supportive role more sustainably and effectively as they become more self-confident and improve in their well-being.

Learning to set boundaries is an ongoing and gradual process, but with time and practice, they will have more balanced and satisfying relationships, both for themselves and others.

Balancing giving and receiving

As generous and other-oriented people, Helpers are often more comfortable giving and providing support than receiving help or attention for themselves. However, for their well-being and to maintain healthy relationships, they need to learn to properly balance giving and receiving.

This balance involves recognizing the importance of self-care. Helpers must understand that taking care of themselves is not selfish, but an essential part of maintaining their well-being and their ability to help others.

This involves dedicating some of your time to rest, nurturing yourself both emotionally and physically, and establishing healthy boundaries in relationships.

Setting boundaries will allow them to conserve their energy and resources for situations where they can be more effective and ensure that their help is genuine and not a negative pattern.

Helpers can practice the art of receiving help and support from others. Learning to receive involves being humble, vulnerable and willing to let others be involved in your life. Allowing others to support them is not only an improvement for themselves, it also strengthens their relationships.

They can also reflect on their relationships and assess whether there is a healthy balance between giving and receiving. They can consider whether they feel valued, supported and listened to in their relationships, as well as whether they are willing to ask for help when they need it.

Identifying imbalances gives them the opportunity to establish open and honest conversations with the important people in their lives.

Balancing giving and receiving is fundamental to emotional well-being and healthy type two relationships. By developing this skill, they discover that self-compassion and self-care are essential to their well-being and their ability to help others in a healthy and sustainable way.

CHAPTER 5

Personality Type 3: The Achiever

Enneagram type threes are characterized by their focus on success, image and achievement. They are ambitious, goal-oriented and highly motivated to achieve recognition and admiration from others.

Achievers are people who are highly focused on success and goal achievement, always achievement-oriented and seeking recognition to validate their worth.

They have a great ability to adapt to different situations and roles, which allows them to excel in different areas of life, such as work, studies or sports.

Achievers tend to be very conscious of their image and how they are perceived by others. They usually strive to project an image of success and perfection at all times.

Their self-esteem and sense of worth are closely linked to external achievements and the approval of others. They may feel empty, or worthless if they do not achieve their goals or receive recognition.

But, behind this mask of success, Achievers often experience a sense of disconnection from their true selves. They may have sacrificed their own authentic desires in pursuit of external approval and recognition.

The constant pursuit of achievement and preoccupation with image can cause Achievers to feel trapped in a rut of performance and inauthenticity, and they can even lose sight of who they really are and what they really want in life.

The pressure to maintain their facade of success can be exhausting for Achievers, as they may feel compelled to constantly meet external expectations and avoid showing vulnerability or failure.

Practicing vulnerability and allowing themselves to show their true selves, even with their imperfections, will allow them to build more genuine and authentic relationships.

Achievers can develop greater self-acceptance, learning to value and appreciate themselves for who they are beyond their accomplishments, is fundamental to cultivating authenticity and inner connection.

It is important for Achievers to allow themselves to connect with their true desires, emotions and needs. This involves questioning and reflecting on what really matters to them and brings them joy beyond external expectations.

Type Threes can find a greater sense of authenticity by setting goals that are aligned with their personal values, rather than solely pursuing external recognition.

We have seen how Achievers, through self-exploration, acceptance and goal setting aligned with their values, as well as setting healthy boundaries, can break free from external expectations and find greater inner connection and authenticity in their lives.

In doing so, they will experience greater personal satisfaction, more authentic relationships and a deeper sense of purpose on their path to personal growth.

Type three personality

Achievers are success-oriented, ambitious and motivated individuals. They are driven by the need to be admired and recognized for their achievements.

Let's look at the distinctive characteristics, motivations and behavioral patterns of this personality type, and how this influences the way they interact with the world and relationships.

Los Triunfadores are characterized by having:

Carefully constructed image: Achievers are adept at projecting an image of success and achievement. They are highly conscious of their public image and strive to present themselves in a flawless and successful manner.

Ambition and competitiveness: They are driven by the desire to stand out and excel in everything they do. They are highly competitive and set ambitious goals to achieve success and gain recognition.

Adaptability: They are able to adapt to different situations and roles to impress others and achieve their goals. They are very adept at reading the expectations of others and adjusting their behavior accordingly.

Results-oriented: They are focused on results and tend to measure their worth by their achievements. They constantly seek new opportunities and challenges to prove their worth and gain external recognition.

Image hypervigilance: They may spend a lot of time and energy on maintaining an image of success and perfection. This can lead them to overexert themselves and put undue pressure on themselves.

Tendency to superficiality: Because of their focus on external success, Achievers may neglect their inner world and emotions. They may appear superficial or emotionally disconnected.

Difficulty relaxing: Achievers may have difficulty relaxing and enjoying the present moment. Their constant drive for achievement can make it difficult for them to enjoy moments of rest and simply be themselves.

On the other hand, Los Triunfadores are usually motivated by:

Obtain recognition and admiration: Type Threes constantly seek recognition and admiration from others. Their self-esteem and sense of personal worth are closely tied to external approval and praise for their accomplishments.

Avoiding failure and mediocrity: They have a deep fear of failure and of being considered mediocre. Their desire to excel drives them to constantly strive and work hard to avoid any form of failure or criticism.

In terms of their interaction with the world and their relationships with others, people with this personality type are noted for:

Focus on impressing others: Achievers tend to put a great deal of effort into impressing others and winning their admiration. This can lead them to make decisions based on external expectations and to neglect their own needs and desires.

Ability to influence and motivate others: They are charismatic and persuasive, which allows them to influence others and motivate them toward the achievement of common goals. They are natural leaders and excellent at inspiring others to reach their full potential.

Difficulty showing vulnerability: Because of their focus on image and success, Achievers may have difficulty showing vulnerability and asking for help. They prefer to maintain a facade of strength and competence, which can make it difficult to establish deep emotional connections.

Some strategies that Los Triunfadores can employ to find authenticity are:

Recognizing one's inner worth: Learning to value and appreciate themselves beyond external achievements and the approval of others. This involves working on cultivating a strong self-esteem and recognizing their intrinsic value as individuals.

Connect with one's emotions: It is important for Achievers to connect with their emotions and allow themselves to experience them rather than suppress or ignore them. This involves cultivating the ability to recognize and express their feelings authentically.

Set meaningful goals and values: Achievers can find authenticity by setting goals and values that are aligned with their true desires and passions. This involves making decisions based on what really matters to them rather than just seeking external recognition.

Practice vulnerability and honesty: Achievers must allow themselves to be vulnerable and share their struggles and weaknesses with others. This will help them build more authentic and meaningful relationships based on trust and mutual honesty.

Type three relationships

The Achiever is known for his focus on success and image, which can influence the way he interacts in different situations.

Let's look at the typical characteristics and behaviors of Achievers in their personal and professional relationships, and how they can improve their connection with themselves and others.

In terms of their personal relationships type three people are characterized by:

Seeking admiration: Achievers often strive for the admiration and recognition of others in their personal relationships. They may tend to show only their successful side and hide their deepest vulnerabilities and emotions.

A Winner, for example, might focus on presenting an impeccable image in their romantic relationships or showing professional accomplishments and avoiding sharing their fears or insecurities.

Competitiveness: Because of their desire to stand out and succeed, Achievers may be competitive in their personal relationships, either overtly or subtly. This can affect relationship dynamics and create tensions.

For example, a type three might feel the need to compete with siblings in terms of achievement, social recognition, or physical appearance.

Adaptability: Achievers tend to adapt to the expectations of others in order to maintain a positive image and be accepted. They may sacrifice their own needs and desires to ensure that others are satisfied and see them as successful and competent.

With respect to their professional relationships, they are characterized by:

Ambition and focus on success: Achievers are known for their ambition and their pursuit of success in the professional arena. They can be tireless and dedicated workers, willing to take on additional responsibilities to achieve their goals.

An Achiever may set ambitious career goals and work hard to obtain promotions, recognition and prestige.

Influence: Achievers have a strong ability to influence and motivate others in the work environment. They can be charismatic and persuasive leaders, able to inspire their colleagues and collaborators to achieve outstanding results.

An Achiever could be a manager or team leader who motivates and leads subordinates to success by setting clear goals and providing support and recognition.

Concern for image and reputation: Achievers tend to take great care of their professional image and reputation. They may be meticulous in the presentation of their work and strive to maintain an impeccable reputation.

An Achiever may spend extra time and effort in preparing presentations or reports to ensure that they reflect his or her professional excellence and perfection.

With respect to the relationship he/she has with him/herself, a Triunfador is characterized by:

Disconnection with their emotions: Achievers often have difficulty connecting with their deepest emotions due to their focus on external success. It is important that they learn to recognize and express their feelings in order to have a more authentic relationship with themselves.

An Achiever might practice introspection and emotional self-exploration, allowing himself or herself to feel and express emotions such as sadness or vulnerability.

Acceptance of vulnerability: Achievers may have difficulty accepting and showing their vulnerability, as they fear it may undermine their image of success. Learning to accept and embrace their vulnerable side will allow them greater authenticity and connection with themselves.

A Winner could confidently share his or her challenges and weaknesses with people he or she trusts, recognizing that being vulnerable does not imply weakness, but strength.

To improve their relationship with others, a type three personality can:

Practice empathic listening: Achievers can become so focused on themselves and their goals that they sometimes neglect to genuinely listen to others. Practicing empathic listening will allow them to build more authentic and meaningful relationships.

An Achiever might devote time and full attention to actively listening to loved ones or colleagues, demonstrating a genuine interest in their concerns and perspectives.

Delegating and relying on others: Achievers tend to take on too much responsibility for fear that others will not meet their expectations. Learning to delegate tasks and trusting in the ability of others will allow them to unburden themselves and strengthen collaborative relationships.

A Winner may assign responsibilities to members of his or her team, giving them the opportunity to grow and demonstrate their competence.

Value personal time and balance: Achievers can be so focused on success and work that they neglect their own well-being and personal time. Learning to set healthy boundaries and making time for self-care will allow them to maintain more balanced and satisfying relationships.

An Achiever might set aside time in his or her schedule for leisure, relaxation and self-care activities, recognizing that work-life balance is critical to his or her overall well-being.

Liberation from the constant search for success

The Achiever, in his tendency to be constantly seeking success, can affect his emotional well-being and his relationships, but he has within his reach several strategies that can help him to free himself from this obsessive search and find a healthier balance in life.

Its cycle of the search for success consists of:

Need for external validation: Achievers have a strong need for external validation and recognition. They constantly seek to prove their worth through accomplishments and goals achieved.

An Achiever may feel dissatisfied unless he receives praise or recognition for his achievements, even if he is not entirely pleased internally.

Self-demand and perfectionism: Achievers tend to impose high standards and expectations on themselves, constantly striving for perfection in everything they do.

An Achiever can put in extra hours at work to make sure their project is flawless and can be recognized for it, even if that means sacrificing time with family or personal rest.

Dependence on results: Achievers tend to link their self-esteem and self-worth to the results obtained. Lack of success or recognition can lead them to feel inadequate or unsuccessful.

An Achiever may experience deep disappointment and frustration if he or she fails to achieve a goal or if his or her performance does not meet expectations.

To free themselves from the constant search for success, type threes can:

Recognize internal self-validation: Achievers can begin to free themselves from the constant search for success by recognizing that their worth does not depend exclusively on external achievements. Learning to value themselves independently of results allows them to find greater emotional stability.

An Achiever can remind himself that his worth is not determined by the recognition of others, but by his own self-perception and self-acceptance.

Set realistic and meaningful goals: Instead of focusing solely on external achievements, Achievers can begin to set goals that are aligned with their values and life purpose. These more meaningful goals allow them to find a sense of inner satisfaction and fulfillment.

An Achiever may set goals that involve contributing to the community, developing personal skills or strengthening meaningful relationships rather than just seeking professional or material achievements.

Cultivate balance and self-care: Achievers need to learn to balance their efforts for success with self-care and time to rest and recharge. Prioritizing self-care helps them maintain proper physical and mental health.

An Achiever could set clear boundaries in their schedule to ensure they have time for activities that promote their well-being, such as exercise, meditation or quality time with loved ones.

On the other hand, the practice of gratitude and appreciation can also be beneficial to Los Triunfadores:

Instead of focusing only on what has yet to be achieved, Achievers can practice gratitude and appreciation for what they have already accomplished. Recognizing and appreciating their past accomplishments helps them find a sense of satisfaction and contentment in the present.

A Triumphator can keep a gratitude journal and write down three things each day for which he or she is grateful, whether big or small.

On the other hand, by recognizing the value of relationships and human connection. They can find a healthy balance by recognizing that success is not only based on individual achievement, but also on meaningful relationships and connections with others. Cultivating authentic relationships and nurturing personal bonds will bring them a sense of fulfillment and emotional satisfaction.

Achievers can find a path to a more balanced and fulfilling life by recognizing the importance of internal self-validation, setting meaningful goals, cultivating balance and self-care, practicing gratitude and valuing relationships.

They can also devote time and effort to strengthening their personal relationships, genuinely connecting with others and expressing their appreciation and love.

By freeing themselves from the constant need for external success, they can discover greater authenticity and happiness on their path to personal growth.

Connecting with authenticity

Achievers are success- and public image-oriented individuals, so they tend to define their worth in terms of achievement and the approval of others.

They are motivated by the desire to stand out, achieve recognition and reach significant goals, so they constantly seek external validation to maintain their successful image.

Behind their apparent success, they often face challenges, as they can become workaholics and overexert themselves. For example, they may sacrifice their personal time or neglect their relationships to devote themselves entirely to their professional career.

They often disconnect from their true authenticity in their eagerness to maintain an image. They may adopt masks and roles that conform to the expectations of others, losing sight of who they really are at their core.

This disconnection from their authenticity can generate a deep sense of emptiness and lack of inner satisfaction, despite their external achievements.

Reconnecting with their authenticity involves a journey of self-exploration and self-acceptance. It is essential that they learn to value themselves for who they are and not just for what they achieve.

Some practices that can help them on this path include introspective reflection, seeking purpose beyond external success, and cultivating authentic and meaningful relationships.

Type Threes can learn to balance their desire for external success with cultivating their authenticity. This involves ceasing to look externally for validation and learning to recognize and value their own qualities as well as their internal accomplishments.

It also involves setting healthy boundaries and learning to say "enough is enough" when necessary, avoiding overexertion and burnout.

Connecting with authenticity is an essential process for Achievers. It gives them the opportunity to live from a place of inner congruence and experience greater satisfaction and fulfillment in their lives.

Through reflection, self-acceptance and the establishment of healthy boundaries, Achievers can free themselves from the constant search for external success and find a balance between their personal goals and their authenticity.

Some examples of how Achievers can apply this in their daily lives include:

Practice self-reflection: Taking time to reflect on their values, interests and passions can help

Achievers connect with their true authenticity. They can do this through journaling, meditation, or simply dedicating moments of silence and quiet to explore their inner world.

Setting healthy boundaries: They tend to say "yes" to many responsibilities and commitments to prove their worth. Learning to set boundaries and say "no" when necessary allows them to prioritize their well-being and devote time and energy to activities that truly fulfill them.

Cultivate authentic relationships: They may seek relationships based on authenticity and reciprocity. This involves seeking out people who accept and value them for who they are beyond their external accomplishments. By surrounding themselves with genuine and supportive people, Achievers can feel more authentic and experience a deeper sense of connection.

Finding purpose beyond success: They can explore their life purpose beyond external achievements. They can ask themselves what they are truly passionate about and how they can contribute to the world in a meaningful way. By aligning their goals with their authenticity, they can find a deeper sense of fulfillment and satisfaction.

Type Threes can free themselves from the constant search for success by connecting with their authenticity, and by reflecting, setting healthy boundaries and finding purpose beyond external achievements, they can have greater inner satisfaction and live a more authentic and fulfilling life.

CHAPTER 6

Personality type 4: The Individualist

Type fours are sensitive, creative and emotional people with a deep need to be unique and authentic; this drives them to seek uniqueness and authenticity in an attempt to find a complete identity.

They often struggle with feelings of dissatisfaction and longing, which can lead them to experience a constant sense of emotional emptiness from focusing on what they lack rather than appreciating what they already have or overlooking the positive things in their lives.

In this chapter, we will discover how type fours can cultivate gratitude as a powerful tool for finding greater joy and fulfillment in their lives.

Cultivating gratitude can be a challenge for The Individualists, as they are often drawn to melancholy and emotional intensity.

They usually face some obstacles, such as comparison with others, the tendency to idealize what is absent, and difficulty recognizing blessings in the midst of pain.

However, with practice and awareness, type fours can learn to open themselves to gratitude and experience its benefits for their personal growth.

It is important for type fours to integrate gratitude as an ongoing practice in their daily lives. To form this habit, they can create visual reminders or establish regular routines in order to reflect on the things they are grateful for.

Gratitude is a powerful antidote to dissatisfaction and longing for Individualists, as it helps them recognize the blessings and positive experiences that are already present in their lives.

Appreciating what they already have and being more grateful will allow them to connect more deeply with themselves and others, finding beauty in their uniqueness and embracing their authenticity in a more balanced and satisfying way.

Gratitude is for them, a powerful tool for self-discovery and authenticity. Through its constant practice, type fours can free themselves from the feeling of emotional emptiness and find greater fulfillment in their lives.

Type four personality

Type fours are known as "The Individualists" or also as "The Romantics" as they are characterized by their deep sensitivity and their constant search for meaning and beauty in the world.

They are highly creative and emotionally expressive, able to connect deeply with their own emotions and those of others.

However, they also have a tendency to experience a deep sense of emotional lack or emptiness, often feeling different and disconnected from others, which can lead them to constantly seek fulfillment in relationships, experiences or artistic expression.

In relationships, type fours crave deep and authentic connection. They seek to be understood and valued by those around them, and can be very sensitive to any signs of rejection or lack of attention.

They find satisfaction in intimate relationships where they feel understood and accepted in their uniqueness. However, it is also important for them to learn to balance their need to be special with the acceptance that all human beings have their own uniqueness and intrinsic value.

For them, personal growth involves learning to manage their emotional intensity and sense of lack. To help improve this aspect, they can practice self-analysis and acceptance of all facets of their being, even those they might label as "dark" or consider "unacceptable."

Type fours can also work on developing a sense of gratitude for what they already have in their lives. By focusing on blessings and positive experiences, they can counteract feelings of emptiness and find greater satisfaction in the present.

One example of how Individualists can manifest their personality in everyday life is through their creative expression. Another example of how they manifest their personality is the way they relate to others. They can be very sensitive to changes in interpersonal dynamics, easily perceiving any lack of connection or attention.

Analyzing their personality allows us to better understand Los Individualistas and their search for authenticity and meaning in life.

By accepting their own uniqueness, cultivating gratitude and developing healthy relationships, type fours can find emotional balance and live a fuller, more authentic life.

Emotionality in the life of type four

Type fours are highly sensitive and emotional people. Their emotions are an integral part of their daily experience. Understanding how this emotionality influences the way they are and how they can manage it in a healthy way is critical to their personal growth.

Individualists are known for their ability to experience a wide range of emotions in a deep and intense way. They can immerse themselves in their feelings and find beauty in the most complex emotions, such as sadness, melancholy and longing.

Their emotional richness allows them to have a unique view of the world and to express themselves through art, music or writing. This sensitivity allows them to connect deeply with others, but can also make them vulnerable to criticism and easily hurt.

Type Four's are extremely sensitive to their own and others' emotions. They can pick up subtle changes in people's moods and are empathetic to the emotional experiences of others. Their emotionality is one of the most, if not the most, important aspect of Type Four identity formation.

They may often feel different or excluded, so they seek to stand out through their uniqueness and strive to be authentic by trying to find a sense of belonging in the expression of their true self.

Managing emotions is a challenge for this Enneagram personality type. Because their emotions are so intense, they may experience more pronounced emotional ups and downs than other personality types.

This is why it is so important that they learn to channel their emotions in a healthier way and to seek emotional balance through self-understanding and self-care.

Type Four's emotionality is often reflected in their creative expression. Many Individualists find art, music, dance or other forms of creative expression an outlet to channel and shape their emotions.

These activities allow them to process and communicate their deepest feelings, and can be a source of inspiration and healing for them.

In an interpersonal relationship, fours can be highly sensitive to emotional changes in their partner or friends. They have the ability to quickly detect if someone is sad, angry or worried, and can offer comfort and emotional support.

However, emotional intensity can also present challenges for type four. Learning to manage these emotional fluctuations and seeking balance is critical to their well-being.

Cultivating self-understanding and acceptance of one's emotions is an important part of personal growth for type four individuals. Learning to recognize and validate their feelings without judging themselves allows them to develop their emotionality in a healthy way and find greater emotional stability.

Type Four's ability to experience emotions deeply and their sensitivity to the emotional experiences of others definitely sets them apart. By understanding and managing their emotions in a healthy way, type fours will be able to have a more authentic connection with themselves and others.

It is important that they know how to take advantage of creative expression, self-understanding, gratitude and emotional balance, as these are key elements to achieve their satisfaction on the path to authenticity.

Fostering gratitude

Type fours are known for their sensitivity and deep connection to their emotions. However, they can sometimes fall into the trap of melancholy and dissatisfaction.

Learning to cultivate gratitude can be a powerful tool for them to find their emotional balance and live a fuller, more satisfying life.

Type fours have a natural tendency to look for the unique and special in the world. They can appreciate the beauty in the little things and find inspiration in what others might overlook.

However, this constant search for uniqueness can lead them to fall into a state of permanent dissatisfaction, as they will always be looking for something that will fulfill them completely. This is where the practice of gratitude can make a big difference.

Individualists tend to focus on what they lack or what they believe makes them different. This can lead them to overlook the blessings and moments of happiness they already have in their lives; in this case, practicing gratitude involves shifting the focus to the positive and valuing what they already have.

In practice, a four can develop gratitude by making a daily list of three things they are grateful for, such as small things like a meaningful conversation, a song that made them feel intense emotions, or a delicious meal.

Type fours often experience intense emotions and may face emotional challenges in their lives. Instead of getting stuck in sadness or frustration, gratitude will allow them to find value and lessons in those difficult experiences.

An Individualist may find gratitude in reflecting on a painful experience and realizing how it has helped him or her grow, become stronger, and better understand self and others.

Expressing gratitude towards others may also help the four in their personal development; they are known for their sensitivity and their ability to empathize with others; thus, by expressing gratitude towards those around them, they can strengthen their emotional connections and foster deeper and more meaningful relationships.

A four may express gratitude to a close friend or loved one for their unconditional support, comforting presence, or ability to understand his or her emotional world.

It is important to note that the path to gratitude may take time and effort for Individualists, as their emotionally intense nature can lead them to fall into negative thought patterns or self-pity.

However, with perseverance and practice, they will be able to develop a more positive and appreciative attitude towards themselves and their environment.

Some additional strategies that can help type fours foster gratitude include keeping a gratitude journal, practicing mindfulness to enjoy simple experiences, and looking for opportunities to express gratitude toward others.

Through the consistent practice of gratitude, type fours can find greater emotional balance, a greater appreciation for the beauty in everyday life, and a deeper connection to their authenticity.

Gratitude gives them the opportunity to find joy and meaning in every moment, opening the way to a fuller and more enriching life.

With these actions, Individualists can break the cycle of dissatisfaction and find a greater appreciation for the blessings and experiences of everyday life, as well as open themselves to the possibility of greater happiness, emotional connection and authenticity.

Thus, gratitude becomes a powerful tool to transform the perspective of the type four and with this, find joy in each of their moments.

Overcoming the tendency to melancholy

Type fours are known for their rich emotional life and their ability to immerse themselves in intense moods, but they can also be prone to falling into the trap of melancholy, where they feel trapped in feelings of sadness, nostalgia and longing.

Throughout this chapter, we will learn effective strategies for type fours to manage and overcome this tendency, and thus find greater emotional balance and well-being.

Melancholy is distinctive to this personality type, and often stems from their innate desire to be unique and special. Individualists may feel a deep sense of loss as if something essential is missing in their lives.

This melancholy can manifest itself in different ways, from sadness and longing for times gone by to a constant sense of dissatisfaction and a feeling that they do not fit into the world. To overcome this tendency to melancholy, it is essential to realize that your emotions do not define you completely.

Individualists can learn to observe and understand their feelings without getting caught up in them. Here are some practical strategies that can help them in this process:

Cultivate emotional awareness: Type fours can develop greater awareness of their emotions and learn to identify when they are slipping into the blues. This allows them to stop and take action to prevent themselves from becoming completely immersed in those feelings.

Finding emotional balance: It is important for type fours to work on balancing their emotions, allowing themselves to feel both sadness and joy. Sometimes, they can be so immersed in melancholy that they fail to recognize the positive experiences in life. Practicing gratitude and focusing on the good things that happen to them can be a great help in counteracting the tendency to melancholy.

Seeking beauty in everyday life: Type Fours have a special sensitivity to appreciating beauty in the world. They can focus on finding moments of beauty in the little things of everyday life, whether it's a landscape, a work of art, or an inspirational song. This allows them to find moments of joy and meaning, counteracting melancholy.

Practice self-reflection: Type fours can benefit from self-reflection and self-awareness. By understanding their emotional patterns and how melancholy can affect their well-being, they can make more conscious decisions to maintain a healthy emotional state.

Seek emotional support: Having a support system of friends, family or professionals can be a great help to type fours. These people can offer an objective perspective and remind type fours of their strengths and accomplishments, helping them find a healthier emotional balance.

Emotional support can offer them a safe space to share their feelings and receive the support they need to overcome the tendency to become melancholy.

Accept their uniqueness. In addition to these strategies, it is critical that type fours give themselves permission to be themselves. Often, melancholy arises from the feeling of not fitting in, but type fours can learn to embrace their individuality and find value in it. Recognizing that we are all unique beings with our own experiences and perspectives can help them break free from the trap of the blues and find a sense of belonging and acceptance.

It is important to note that overcoming the tendency to melancholy can take time and effort. Each individual is different, and the process of cultivating gratitude and finding emotional balance may vary.

However, with practice and determination, type fours can learn to live a fuller life, appreciating beauty and finding meaning in every experience.

By learning to appreciate the uniqueness of their being and finding gratitude in every aspect of life, type fours can free themselves from melancholy and live a more authentic and fulfilling life.

This process not only benefits their emotional well-being, but also allows them to connect more deeply with themselves and others.

CHAPTER 7

Personality type 5: The Observer

Type fives value knowledge, independence and privacy. They have a natural inclination toward analytical thinking and information seeking, but can often have difficulty connecting emotionally with others and balancing their focus on knowledge with intimacy and meaningful relationships.

Observers are highly intellectual people who seek deep understanding of the world around them. They have a tendency to withdraw emotionally and maintain their privacy, as they value their independence and personal space.

They are often more comfortable in solitary settings or with a small circle of intimate people rather than large social groups.

They may have difficulty expressing and understanding their own emotions, as well as connecting emotionally with others. It is common for them to feel overwhelmed by emotional intensity and choose to distance themselves, or retreat into the world of knowledge, to avoid facing their feelings.

This lack of emotional connection can affect their relationships and make it difficult to create intimate and meaningful bonds; however, type fives can develop emotional connection by practicing self-awareness and acceptance of their own feelings.

It is important that they allow themselves to experience and express emotions without judging themselves. They can explore creative activities or expressive therapies as a means to safely connect with their emotions.

Learning to communicate openly and honestly about your feelings with people you trust is also critical to developing emotional connection.

They can learn to balance their desire for knowledge with the need for intimacy and meaningful relationships by seeking opportunities to share their knowledge and perspectives with others, enabling them to contribute meaningfully in social interactions.

A type five might spend time researching and gaining an in-depth understanding of a topic they are passionate about, but would also challenge themselves to share that knowledge with others in an academic setting or discussion group.

Practicing empathy and genuine interest in the experiences and emotions of others can also help them build deeper connections.

A type five might explore creative activities such as writing, painting, or music as a way to express and connect with his or her own emotions, and might join a workshop or artists' group to share his or her creations and emotions with others.

In a personal situation, a type five might practice emotional openness by sharing their concerns or joys with a close friend or loved one, allowing themselves to connect on a deeper level.

During a work meeting, an Observer might strive to actively listen to others' ideas and perspectives, showing genuine interest in their experiences and emotions, allowing them to make more meaningful connections in the work environment.

By finding a balance between knowledge and intimacy, type fives can expand their ability to connect emotionally with themselves and others, as well as enjoy more rewarding relationships.

Type five personality

The type five personality is characterized by a desire to acquire knowledge, observation and a tendency to withdraw emotionally.

Let's look at the characteristics, motivations and typical behaviors of this type, as well as strategies for Observers to develop deeper and more satisfying emotional connections in their lives.

Type Fives are thoughtful and reserved individuals who value privacy and time alone to recharge their batteries. They have an innate curiosity and a constant desire to acquire knowledge in areas that interest them.

They tend to be detailed observers, analytical and deep in their thinking, preferring solitude and seeking quiet spaces to process their thoughts.

They seek to preserve their energy and protect their privacy, which leads them to establish clear boundaries with others. They need to have a broad knowledge and understanding of the world in order to feel secure and competent.

However, they may experience a sense of scarcity in relation to their time, energy and resources, leading them to withdraw emotionally as a measure of self-protection.

Type fives may be selective in their relationships, preferring the company of people with similar interests or who respect their need for space and time alone. This can create an apparent emotional distance and make it difficult to connect intimately with others.

They sometimes have difficulty expressing their emotions and needs, which can cause misunderstandings and frustrations in relationships. However, when they feel secure and respected, they can provide a deep level of intellectual and emotional support to their loved ones.

To develop a healthier emotional connection, they can work on recognizing and expressing their own emotions. Practicing active and empathic listening will help them connect emotionally with others.

Participating in activities that stimulate creativity and emotional expression, such as art, music or writing, will allow them to connect with themselves and their emotions in a more conscious way.

By sharing their knowledge and experiences with others, type fives can establish meaningful connections based on mutual exchange.

Through openness and willingness to share their wisdom, they can make a valuable contribution to their relationships and find a balance between their desire for privacy and their need for emotional connection.

By better understanding type fives and strategies for cultivating their emotional connection, we can appreciate and nurture relationships with the type fives in our lives.

Interaction with the emotional world

Type fives tend to be reserved and guarded about their own emotions. Because of their focus on acquiring knowledge and their desire to preserve their privacy, they can become emotionally disconnected and appear distant or cold. However, it is important to keep in mind that they do not lack emotions; they just handle them differently.

Type fives tend to have a broad emotional spectrum, but often prefer to observe and analyze their emotions rather than express them openly. This may be due to their desire to protect their personal space and maintain a sense of control over their emotions. They may be more comfortable processing their feelings internally rather than sharing them with others.

In emotionally charged situations, type fives may choose to withdraw further, seeking solitude and alone time to process their emotions. They may devote long hours to personal research and reflection to better understand their feelings and find logical solutions.

This approach can be beneficial in certain respects, as type fives tend to be deeply reflective individuals and have an innate ability to analyze complex situations. However, the tendency of type fives to withdraw emotionally can make it difficult to connect intimately with others.

They may have difficulty expressing their emotions openly and may be seen as distant or unapproachable by those seeking a deeper emotional connection.

In order for type fives to develop a fuller emotional connection, it is important that they give themselves permission to explore and express their emotions in healthy ways.

Here are some strategies that can help you in this process:

Emotional self-awareness: Type fives can benefit from spending time identifying and understanding their own emotions. They can keep an emotional journal to record their feelings and reflect on them. In addition, they can practice mindfulness and mindful observation of their emotional states in different situations.

Assertive communication: Although it can be challenging, type fives can learn to express their emotions clearly and respectfully. They can practice assertive communication by sharing their feelings directly, avoiding the tendency to repress or minimize their emotions.

Seeking emotional support: It is important for type fives to seek emotional support in their environment. They can rely on trusted people with whom they can feel comfortable sharing their emotions. These people can be close friends, family members, or even therapists or counselors. By opening up to others, type fives can experience greater emotional connection and feel supported in their personal development process.

Practice empathy: Although type fives may have difficulty connecting emotionally with others, it is important for them to practice empathy. They can strive to understand others' emotions and put themselves in their shoes. This will help them develop greater emotional sensitivity and make more authentic and meaningful connections.

Seeking Balance: While it is valuable for Type Fives to spend time in their inner world and in their quest for knowledge, it is also important for them to find a healthy balance between introspection and connecting with others. They can engage in social activities and participate in activities that allow them to share emotional experiences with others.

Let's imagine a guy five named Javier, he is a scientific researcher who spends most of his time in his lab, immersed in his intellectual work, and lately, he has noticed that his tendency to withdraw emotionally has led him to feel disconnected from his loved ones and to experience a sense of loneliness.

Javier decides to apply some of the above strategies. He begins to keep an emotional diary in which he records his feelings and reflects on them at the end of each day. In addition, he commits to communicating more openly about his emotions to his partner and close friends.

Javier also seeks emotional support by sharing his concerns and challenges with a therapist. Through these conversations, he learns to practice empathy by better-understanding others' emotions and how they can affect his relationships.

Gradually, Javier finds a balance between his intellectual work and his emotional life. He begins to participate in social activities and becomes more involved in shared experiences with his loved ones. As he opens up emotionally, he experiences a greater connection with others and a sense of fulfillment in his life.

Type fives may face challenges in emotional connection due to their tendency to withdraw and focus on knowledge acquisition. However, through the practice of emotional self-awareness, assertive communication, seeking emotional support, empathy and balance, type fives can develop a deeper connection with their own emotions and with others. In doing so, they will experience greater satisfaction and fulfillment in their relationships and in their lives in general.

Overcoming emotional isolation

Let's imagine a young woman named Laura, who identifies with the type five personality. She is a graduate student in physics and is used to spending long hours researching and immersing herself in her intellectual world. However, she has realized that she has been avoiding expressing and exploring her own emotions, which has led to an emotional disconnect with the people around her.

To overcome emotional isolation, Laura decides to take concrete steps. First, she begins to practice emotional self-awareness. She takes time to reflect on her own emotions, even the most uncomfortable or intense ones. In addition, through meditation and writing, Laura allows herself to experience and better understand her feelings.

Next, Laura challenges herself to communicate her emotions to others. She begins by sharing her thoughts and feelings with her best friend, opening up in a way she has never done before.

As she becomes more comfortable expressing her emotions, Laura notices how her connection with her friend grows stronger and how they can both support each other in a deeper way.

In addition, Laura seeks emotional support in discussion groups and therapy. She finds a group of people with similar interests where she can talk openly about her emotional experiences and challenges. She also decides to seek the help of a therapist to guide her toward greater emotional connection.

Over time, Laura finds that cultivating empathy and emotional connection becomes more natural to her. She becomes involved in activities that allow her to understand and share the emotions of others, such as participating in community projects and attending cultural events.

As she opens up to the emotional experiences of others, Laura discovers a new depth in her relationships and a fuller sense of satisfaction in her life.

Through self-awareness, open communication, emotional support and the practice of empathy, type fives can break the cycle of isolation and experience a more meaningful emotional connection with others.

By practicing gratitude towards their own emotions and recognizing their importance in life, Observers can find a balance between their intellect and their emotional world, enjoying richer relationships and greater personal satisfaction.

Overcoming emotional isolation is a process that requires time and effort, but it is possible.

Type fives can learn to balance their intellectual focus with a deeper emotional connection, allowing them to enjoy more meaningful relationships and greater fulfillment in their lives.

Developing connection with others

Type fives are highly intellectual and seek to understand the world through the accumulation of knowledge and observation. However, because of their need for privacy, they may neglect their interpersonal relationships; this orientation can isolate them emotionally and can make it difficult for them to establish intimate and satisfying relationships.

The Observer can cultivate a deeper and more meaningful connection with others. The first step in achieving this is to recognize and value the importance of human relationships. By understanding that these connections are fundamental to well-being and fulfillment, type fives can be motivated to seek ways to develop and maintain meaningful relationships.

An effective way for a type five to cultivate connection with others is to practice active listening. This involves being present in conversations, paying full attention to what the other is saying and showing genuine interest in their perspective.

By being an attentive and sympathetic listener, type fives can demonstrate their commitment to connecting with others and fostering an environment of trust and openness.

For example, imagine John, a type five who is participating in a team meeting at work. Instead of remaining silent and distant, Juan engages in active listening. He asks questions to delve deeper into his teammates' ideas, shows genuine interest in their points of view, and responds in a respectful manner. This active listening attitude helps Juan establish a more meaningful connection with his colleagues and strengthens his relationship in the work environment.

Observers have a wealth of knowledge and interesting experiences to share. Cultivating connection with others involves finding opportunities to share this knowledge and experiences in an accessible and enriching way.

They can contribute to conversations and discussions with insightful ideas, participate in group activities where they can share their skills and offer their help and support to those in need.

For example, Maria, a type five with a passion for history, decides to give a talk in her community about a specific historical period. Through research and preparation, Maria creates an informative and entertaining presentation that she shares with the group. By sharing her knowledge and passion, Maria not only nurtures her own connection to history, but also creates a bond with attendees who share her interest in the topic.

Type fives often have a natural affinity for working independently, but to cultivate a connection with others, it is important that they also seek opportunities for collaboration and teamwork. By joining with others, type fives can benefit from different perspectives, share complementary ideas and skills, and develop stronger relationships based on working together.

For example, Pablo, a guy five who enjoys computer programming, decides to join a team-based software development project. Although he initially feels comfortable working alone, he realizes that by collaborating with other programmers, he can improve his skills, learn new techniques, and contribute more meaningfully to the project.

As he works closely with his colleagues, Pablo also develops closer relationships and feels more connected to the team.

To cultivate emotional connection with others, type fives can benefit from practicing empathy and compassion. This involves putting oneself in others' shoes, trying to understand their experiences and emotions, and showing compassion and genuine support.

By developing greater sensitivity to the needs and feelings of others, type fives can establish more authentic and deeper relationships.

For example, Ana, a type five who tends to be reserved and self-centered, strives to practice empathy in her personal relationships. When her friend Laura tells her about an emotional challenge she is facing, Ana takes the time to listen carefully, validate Laura's feelings, and offer words of support and encouragement.

By demonstrating empathy and compassion, Ana strengthens her connection with Laura and builds a stronger and more meaningful friendship.

Through the practice of active listening, sharing knowledge and experiences, seeking collaboration and teamwork, practicing empathy and compassion, type fives can overcome their tendency to emotional isolation and develop more authentic and satisfying relationships.

In doing so, they find a balance between their need for knowledge and their longing for human connection, allowing them to experience a more fulfilling life.

CHAPTER 8

Personality type 6: The Loyal

Personality type six corresponds to people who are characterized by being loyal, responsible and committed, but because of their concern for safety and their focus on risk avoidance, they may doubt themselves and have difficulty trusting their own judgment.

In this chapter, we will discover the key characteristics of Type Six Loyalists, the challenges they face with regard to self-confidence and the strategies they can employ to overcome them.

Lack of self-confidence can limit type sixes' personal and professional growth, as well as their ability to take healthy risks.

Let's imagine Laura, a type six woman who constantly struggles with her self-confidence. Despite having a stable job, she feels insecure about her ability to advance in her career and is overly dependent on the approval of others. However, she is determined to overcome this limitation and increase her self-confidence.

Laura begins to practice daily self-affirmation, remembering her past accomplishments and strengths before she begins her workday. She also begins to identify the fears that hold her back, such as the fear of failure and the judgment of others. With the support of a coach, Laura gradually challenges these fears by setting more ambitious goals in her work and taking on more challenging projects. As she achieves small successes, her self-confidence grows.

In addition to working on herself, Laura looks for the right support in her work environment. She finds a mentor who has overcome similar challenges and can provide guidance and encouragement. Her mentor encourages her to take calculated risks and trust her intuition. Moreover, Laura surrounds herself with positive friends and colleagues who support her and motivate her to believe in herself.

As Laura continues to advance in her career, her self-confidence continues to grow and she becomes more confident in her own judgment, finally beginning to make decisions with more peace of mind. Although she still faces moments of self-doubt, Laura has freed herself from relying too much on external validation and feels more confident in her ability to face work challenges.

Developing self-confidence is a gradual process for type sixes. By facing fears, practicing self-assertion, seeking appropriate support, and taking progressive steps, they can overcome their tendency toward self-neglect and cultivate solid self-confidence.

In doing so, they experience greater satisfaction and success in all areas of their lives.

Type six personality

Type six is characterized by being loyal, possessing such positive qualities as a sense of duty and commitment to others. They are reliable and concerned about safety.

Their main focus is to protect themselves and their loved ones, which makes them cautious and always alert to possible dangers. However, this excessive worry can lead to anxiety and doubts in their ability to make decisions and trust themselves.

Loyalists constantly seek approval and validation from others. This need for security can lead them to become emotionally dependent on others, which can become excessive at times.

Fear is an important characteristic in type sixes and can manifest itself in different ways; some may become more fearful and cautious, while others may adopt a more defiant and rebellious attitude. However, it is common for all to experience a sense of constant alertness and worry about the future.

Each of Los Leales has a unique way of expressing their personality, so it is important to keep in mind that these characteristics may vary from case to case.

To better understand the type six personality, let's look at an everyday situation. For example, Maria, a type six woman, works in a company and constantly worries about potential problems. Although she is loyal to her team, her need for security can make her indecisive in making important decisions.

Overcoming self-doubt and anxiety is a process that requires self-exploration and personal work. Acknowledging past achievements and successes is an effective strategy to strengthen self-confidence. In addition, fostering self-compassion and acceptance is fundamental, as we all make mistakes and personal growth involves constant learning.

Learning to manage fear and anxiety in a healthy way is another important aspect of developing type six. Practicing relaxation techniques and seeking the support of mental health professionals can be of great help in this case.

In everyday life, we find examples of how they can cultivate self-confidence. Alejandro, a type six man, feels insecure when presenting a project at work. However, through preparation, research and seeking support, he manages to overcome his anxiety and present his project with confidence.

Type Sixes can strengthen their confidence and develop greater security in their abilities. In doing so, they will find greater balance and satisfaction in their lives, establishing a stronger connection with themselves and others.

Struggles and strengths of type six

The type six personality is characterized by loyalty, commitment and concern for security. They are willing to be supportive of those they consider important in their lives. However, they may also experience distrust and overdependence in their relationships, making it difficult to form strong bonds.

One of type six's struggles is distrust, driven by their fear of abandonment and betrayal. They constantly doubt the intentions of others and look for signs of threat. In addition, they can become emotionally over-dependent, constantly seeking approval and validation.

Despite their struggles, type sixes have valuable strengths; their loyalty and commitment make them reliable companions. Their ability to detect threats and anticipate problems is useful in difficult situations, and their concern for security allows them to establish bonds based on trust and mutual protection.

To overcome these struggles, it is critical for type sixes to work on managing their fear and anxiety and building self-confidence. This involves setting healthy boundaries in relationships. Open and honest communication is also key, expressing concerns clearly and respectfully.

An example of how type sixes can develop strengths in relationships is Laura, who seeks therapy to explore her roots of distrust and learn techniques to manage her anxiety. She also commits to setting healthy boundaries and communicating openly with her loved ones. Through this process, she builds a solid foundation of trust and develops her autonomy.

Although they face challenges, type sixes are able to overcome their struggles and build healthier, more meaningful relationships. By cultivating self-confidence, setting boundaries and communicating openly, they find a balance between safety and authentic connection with others.

Overcoming fear

Fear is a fundamental emotion that we have all experienced at some point in our lives. However, for Enneagram type six, fear plays a central role in their personality and can become overwhelming.

To better understand the fear of The Loyalists, I introduce David, a middle-aged man who identifies as a type six. David lives constantly in a state of alert, anticipating the worst and looking for ways to protect himself and his loved ones. His fear manifests itself in a series of worries and catastrophic scenarios that may seem irrational to others, but are very real to him.

One of David's main struggles is the fear of abandonment, based on past experiences of betrayal and feeling left out; this leads him to constantly seek validation and confirmation from others, generating tension in his relationships.

To overcome his fear, David begins working on self-discovery and personal growth. Through therapy and self-examination, he challenges his limiting thoughts and beliefs, questioning the veracity of his fears and exploring healthier ways to approach challenging situations. In addition, you engage in developing greater self-confidence, gradually facing your fears and acquiring new skills to handle difficult situations.

David also builds a strong support network, surrounding himself with people who encourage him to face his fears and give him the emotional support he needs. He learns to manage fear in a healthy and constructive way, recognizing that it can be a sign of caution but not letting it control his life or limit his experiences.

In his journey of overcoming fear, David finds inspiration from other courageous and resilient people. He also practices stress and anxiety management techniques, such as meditation and positive visualization, to calm his mind and make more balanced and rational decisions.

Throughout his process, David discovers that challenges offer opportunities for growth and empowerment. He changes his perspective and sees obstacles as learning experiences rather than imminent threats, approaching them with greater confidence and determination.

Through David's story of struggle and overcoming, we have discovered that through self-examination, coping, finding inspiration and adopting stress management techniques, type sixes can break free from the paralysis of fear and live a fuller, more courageous life.

Developing self-confidence

Type six tends to be cautious and doubt their own abilities, limiting their personal growth and success. To overcome this, it is necessary to consciously self-reflect in order to strengthen their inner confidence and live a more satisfying life.

Exploring past strengths, skills and accomplishments is essential for Loyalists to develop self-confidence. It is essential that they admit and appreciate their own worth and capabilities, and it can be inspiring to recognize how they overcame challenges in the past.

Negative thoughts fuel self-doubt and undermine the self-confidence of type sixes, so it is important that they learn to question and challenge these thoughts; the key is to examine the evidence that supports or refutes them and replace them with more realistic and positive statements.

Working gradually toward achievable goals is an effective way to build self-confidence. Identifying small goals and taking concrete steps toward them can build confidence. In addition, having the support of trusted people, such as friends, family or professionals, provides encouragement, objective perspectives and constructive feedback.

Loyalists can develop their self-confidence by taking on challenges and facing new situations, accepting each experience as an opportunity for learning and growth, even when they have adverse outcomes, as they can use mistakes to learn and improve.

For type sixes, it is also important to recognize and celebrate successes, no matter how small, which boosts their self-confidence and gives them positive momentum. Personal celebration, sharing accomplishments with people they trust, or rewarding themselves in some special way can be effective strategies.

On the other hand, practicing self-compassion, treating each other with kindness and understanding in moments of doubt or self-criticism is essential for personal growth; seeing failures as opportunities to grow will allow The Loyalists to build a solid and lasting trus

Developing self-confidence is a personal and gradual process. By overcoming self-doubt and believing in self-worth, type sixes can face challenges with confidence and live a fuller, more authentic life, tapping into their full potential and enjoying more meaningful and rewarding relationships.

CHAPTER 9

Personality type 7: The Enthusiast

Type Sevens have a vibrant and optimistic personality, are creative and adventurous people who are always in search of new experiences and opportunities and constantly seek fulfillment and excitement in life. However, they also face challenges and struggle to find lasting fulfillment and satisfaction.

Behind their apparent joy and enthusiasm, Enthusiasts have a tendency to avoid pain and emotional discomfort by seeking positive experiences and distractions. This can lead them to escape difficult or emotionally challenging situations.

To find fulfillment in the present, it is important that you recognize this pattern, allow yourself to be present and face the emotions that arise.

Learning to be comfortable with discomfort and facing challenges will help them experience a deeper sense of fulfillment and authenticity.

Constantly seeking new experiences sometimes prevents them from appreciating the simple and beautiful things they already have in their lives. Developing gratitude will allow them to fully appreciate and enjoy what they have in the present.

You can do this by keeping a gratitude journal, and recording three things you are grateful for each day, or by simply taking a moment to reflect on the blessings and joys that already exist in your life.

By practicing gratitude, type sevens find fulfillment in the little things and develop a greater connection to the present moment.

The enthusiastic nature of type seven can lead them to take on too many commitments and fill their life with activities, which disperses their energy and exhausts them.

To find fulfillment in the present, you must learn to set boundaries and say "no" when necessary. This will allow them to devote time and energy to the things that really matter to them and bring them satisfaction.

By setting healthy boundaries, type sevens can find a balance between exploring new experiences and dedication to the things that bring them fulfillment.

The practice of mindfulness is especially beneficial for type sevens, as it helps them to be present in the moment and to fully enjoy each experience.

It involves paying deliberate, nonjudgmental attention to present thoughts, sensations and emotions. Enthusiasts can practice mindfulness in everyday activities such as eating, walking, or sitting quietly for a few minutes a day.

By being present and aware at the moment, type sevens can experience greater wholeness and connection with themselves and their environment.

Another important aspect of finding fulfillment in the present is for type sevens to open up to vulnerability. They often avoid situations that make them feel vulnerable or emotionally exposed.

However, by allowing themselves to feel and express a full range of emotions, even uncomfortable or unpleasant ones, they can experience greater authenticity and a deeper connection with themselves and others.

Type Sevens also have a tendency to live in the future, anticipating new experiences and constantly chasing the next adventure. However, to find fulfillment in the present, it is essential that they focus on the now.

This involves savoring and fully enjoying each experience without projecting too far into the future. They can practice being present at the moment through techniques such as meditation, mindful breathing and mindfulness in daily activities.

The Enthusiast has the ability to find fulfillment in the present by recognizing the impulse to avoid, cultivating gratitude, setting boundaries, practicing mindfulness, embracing vulnerability, and seeking fulfillment in the now.

By developing these skills and perspectives, type sevens can experience greater emotional connection, authenticity and fulfillment in their lives.

As they learn to fully enjoy each moment, they free themselves from the constant search for intense emotions and find deep joy and fulfillment in the present.

Type seven personality

The Enneagram personality type seven is characterized by being energetic, optimistic and pleasure-oriented. They are true adventurers, always on the lookout for new exciting experiences; they love to explore all the possibilities life has to offer and make the most of them.

However, behind their apparent cheerfulness, type sevens have a deep aversion to pain and emotional suffering. They prefer to avoid difficult or unpleasant situations and constantly seek pleasure and escape.

This desire to avoid pain also leads them to constantly seek new experiences and intense emotions, and this attitude drives them to fill their agenda with activities and projects to keep themselves busy and distracted, thus avoiding facing their most difficult emotions.

For them, variety and constant stimulation are vital. They like to have a variety of options and opportunities open to them, as this gives them a sense of security and satisfaction.

They find it difficult to commit to a single choice or a single path in life, as they fear missing out on something better or more exciting in the future.

Despite their energy and contagious joy, Enthusiasts also face challenges in connecting with their own deeper emotions. They often identify with their image as happy, optimistic people, but this can lead them to repress or deny less pleasant emotions such as sadness or fear.

This denial of their emotions can generate a disconnection from their true self and hinder their ability to face the emotional challenges of life, so it is important for them to learn to understand, accept and manage their own emotions.

Behind that cheerful facade, there is also room to experience deep emotions. By allowing themselves to feel and express what they feel, they can find a balance between the pursuit of pleasure and the ability to face emotional challenges. This will allow them to have genuine fulfillment in the present and stay connected to themselves.

Focus on the search for experiences

Type Sevens are energetic, enthusiastic and adventurous, they like to live life to the fullest and this drives them to seek out stimulating experiences. They are tireless explorers, finding fun and excitement in any situation. They seek opportunities, travel, relationships and creative activities that give them pleasure, joy and a sense of freedom.

Sometimes their focus on seeking experiences can lead them to avoid uncomfortable or painful situations, but they prefer to avoid any negative feelings and avoid them. It is important for them to find a healthy balance between seeking satisfying experiences and accepting all facets of life, both positive and negative.

Enthusiasts can learn to face emotional challenges and be present at the moment. In doing so, they will develop greater emotional depth and experience true fulfillment in their lives.

Embracing wholeness in the present

The Enthusiast is characterized by their constant search for exciting experiences, their contagious enthusiasm and their desire to avoid any type of restriction or limitation. However, in their eagerness to find happiness and fulfillment, they have difficulty being fully present at the moment and feel dissatisfied.

Type Sevens tend to be easily distracted by anticipation of future projects, trips or activities, and struggle to stay engaged in the present. To find fulfillment in the present, they need to learn to be aware of their own emotions and needs, and to face the challenges they face.

This involves exploring and accepting both pleasant and difficult experiences, allowing emotions to flow without avoiding or suppressing them.

A type seven can enjoy taking a walk, observing the vibrant colors of the flowers, feeling the breeze on their face, listening to the birds singing and living in the present moment rather than planning their next adventure or distracting themselves with thoughts of future events. An Enthusiast can feel fulfilled and satisfied by being open to the experience and savoring the present.

Type Sevens often worry about missing out on something better, or feeling trapped in long-term commitments. However, they can discover joy in authentic and meaningful relationships by cultivating presence and emotional connection with others.

It is essential that they practice mindfulness and gratitude, which may include appreciating a delicious meal, enjoying an intimate conversation with a loved one, or enjoying peace and quiet.

Type Sevens are challenged to confront and process the fear or discomfort that may arise by stopping and facing their emotions rather than avoiding them. Through introspection, they can overcome their resistance to pain and discover that by allowing themselves to feel full, they can also experience greater joy and satisfaction in their life.

Through mindfulness, gratitude and emotional connection with others, Enthusiasts can learn to be present in their lives, find greater satisfaction in each experience and discover that happiness is found in the ability to enjoy and savor each moment of life.

An example might be a Seven during a party with friends. Instead of constantly thinking about what to do after the party or upcoming activities, she engages in fully enjoying the moment, converses with enthusiasm, laughs with authenticity, and connects emotionally with others, experiencing a sense of fulfillment and genuine connection.

Avoiding dispersion

Enthusiasts jump from one activity to another without fully enjoying each one. This causes them constant dissatisfaction; they are never fully satisfied with what they are doing in the present.

By avoiding dispersion, type sevens can learn to find a balance between their desire for diversity and their ability to be present in the moment. They can achieve this by setting priorities and maintaining a focus on the most meaningful tasks and projects.

By identifying and committing to concrete goals, they will channel their energy and enthusiasm into activities that truly bring them satisfaction and fulfillment.

Mindfulness also helps them to be present in the present moment by observing their thoughts and emotions without getting carried away by them. By becoming aware of their impulses and desires to avoid boredom, type sevens will make more conscious and deliberate decisions about what to focus their time and energy on.

In addition, self-exploration and acceptance of emotional discomfort are critical to finding a balance between the desire for diversity and the ability to be present in the moment.

By confronting underlying fears and exploring their enthusiastic and curious nature, type sevens can adopt strategies to avoid dispersion and cultivate the ability to be fully present in every experience.

A practical example would be an Enthusiast in a work meeting with multiple exciting project opportunities. Instead of committing to all of them right away, he reflects and evaluates which one best aligns with his values and long-term goals. By making a more conscious decision and avoiding dispersion, he can focus on one project at a time and devote his energy and attention fully to that goal.

By overcoming the tendency to scatter, type sevens will be present in every experience and fully engaged in what they choose to do, with a depth to their lives that they have not previously experienced. In addition, by finding a balance between seeking new experiences and the ability to be rooted in the moment, they can develop more meaningful relationships and enjoy a greater connection with others.

CHAPTER 10

Personality type 8: The Protector

Type eights are strong, confident and decisive types who tend to take control in various situations, often facing the challenge of transforming their need for control into healthy and constructive empowerment.

They have an innate strength, but sometimes they can feel the pressure to control everything around them; this generates conflicts and obstacles, both in their relationships and in their life in general.

To develop empowerment rather than control, type eights can begin by becoming aware of their own fears and vulnerabilities, recognizing that their need to control often arises to protect themselves from being hurt or vulnerable.

By being aware of this pattern of behavior, type eights can make more conscious decisions and develop more confidence in their ability to face challenges without being overly controlling.

An example might be an eight who leads a work team. Initially, the Protector may have a tendency to impose his ideas and decisions without considering the opinions of others. However, as he reflects on his own fears of losing control, he may realize that his true strength lies in allowing others to contribute and feel valued. He learns to empower his team by fostering an environment of collaboration and mutual support, leveraging individual strengths and making decisions based on consensus.

They can also benefit from trusting others and delegating responsibilities, recognizing that they do not have to carry all the weight on their shoulders, they can free themselves from the burden of controlling everything, and feel personal freedom and relief.

Delegating responsibilities gives them the opportunity to focus on strategic and more important issues. They feel less overwhelmed, encourage the growth and development of others, and create an environment of collaboration and mutual trust.

Through self-awareness, trust in others and effective delegation, type eights can develop more balanced and empathetic leadership with greater authenticity and satisfaction. By cultivating awareness of their fears and vulnerabilities, trusting and delegating responsibility, type eights can find a healthy balance in their leadership style.

It is important to note that the process of transforming control into empowerment does not happen overnight. It requires constant practice, self-reflection and a willingness to learn from mistakes. Type Eights may find themselves in situations where they are tempted to take back control, especially when faced with challenges or stressful situations.

However, by remembering the goal of empowering others and trusting in their team's potential, they can overcome these obstacles and cultivate stronger relationships.

Type eight personality

The type eight personality is characterized by being strong, energetic and determined, with a desire to control their environment. Type eights are courageous and bold, not afraid to take on leadership and face challenges. They have powerful energy and an inner drive to protect others and defend their own needs and interests.

Behind their strong and dominant appearance, they also have a deep need to be loved and accepted. They have experienced situations that have made them feel vulnerable or have been hurt in the past, which has led them to develop an emotional armor to protect themselves. As a result, they may have difficulty showing their vulnerability and fully trusting others.

They need to control their environment to protect themselves; they adopt a posture of strength and dominance, seeking to be in control in all situations.

While they can be direct and outspoken, openly expressing their opinions and desires, it is important to balance this attitude with openness to vulnerability and empathy for others.

An everyday example of the type eight personality might be the senior corporate executive known for his or her decisiveness and determination in leading projects and making important decisions. While his approach inspires confidence in his team, he may also overlook the ideas and perspectives of others, leading to lack of collaboration and resentment. Immersed in his drive for control, the executive may have difficulty connecting emotionally with colleagues and subordinates, limiting the development of strong, nurturing relationships.

For type eights, it is critical to understand how their need for control affects their relationships and emotional well-being.

Learning to balance their strength and leadership, with a greater openness to vulnerability and empathy, allows them to establish more authentic and satisfying connections with others, developing a more collaborative leadership style and building relationships based on trust and emotional connection.

Relationship with power

This personality type has a strong inclination toward control and dominance, which is reflected in their assertive and decisive approach to all areas of their lives. To better understand this relationship with power, it is important to note that type eights seek power as a way to protect themselves and others.

Imagine a charismatic and determined business leader. This leader has a direct and assertive approach, and is known for making quick and decisive decisions. In challenging situations, he assumes a leadership role and makes sure things are done his way. Although he may appear authoritarian, his underlying goal is to maintain control and safeguard the interests of his team and organization.

As Type Eights seek to control their environment, they often face resistance from others and can generate conflict in their interpersonal relationships. Their need to have the last word and take charge can undermine trust and collaboration in teams and group situations.

Some practical strategies for type eights to develop more inclusive and participative leadership are learning to actively listen to the ideas and perspectives of others, and learning to delegate responsibilities by fostering an environment where everyone feels valued and respected. In this way, they can use their power to build strong relationships and promote positive change in their environment.

Type eights can find a healthy balance in their relationship with power through self-awareness and empathy. With these, they can learn to use their power constructively and empower others rather than subjugate them.

By reflecting on their motivations and considering the impact of their actions on others, type eights can develop more constructive leadership and strengthen interpersonal relationships.

Through practical strategies, such as active listening, delegating responsibility and fostering an inclusive environment, Protectors can transform their relationship with power into a tool for empowering others and promoting positive change.

Relationship to control

The type eight has a strong relationship with control, seeking to protect themselves and others in their drive for independence and autonomy. However, this quest for control can have both positive aspects and challenges.

Type eights tend to be dominant and powerful personalities, which often translates into a desire to have control over their environment and the situations they find themselves in. Control gives them a sense of security and allows them to maintain their independence and autonomy.

However, their drive to control can lead them to be inflexible and reluctant to accept different points of view or suggestions from others. They may resist change and fight against any attempt at outside influence that they perceive as a threat to their power.

Their challenge is to find a healthy balance between being in control and allowing others to have a voice and participation in decisions as well. It is important that they learn to trust others and delegate responsibility.

Type eights can develop a healthier relationship with control by working on developing trust in themselves and others. Learning to let go of excessive control and allowing others to actively participate can strengthen relationships and generate a collaborative environment.

Laura, a type eight, has a strong personality and likes to be in control of her personal life. When her partner suggests changing her plans for the weekend, she is reluctant and defends her original idea, as she finds it difficult to adapt to new proposals.

She is committed to practicing open communication and active listening with her partner to cultivate trust and balance. She recognizes that excessive control can negatively affect their relationship and strives to give her partner space to express his or her opinions and make joint decisions. This creates an environment of mutual respect and strengthens the emotional bond between them.

By learning to let go of excessive control and allowing the active participation of others, the type eight can develop stronger relationships and generate a sense of empowerment for both themselves and those around them.

It is important to find a healthy balance, avoiding rigidity and resistance, and cultivating confidence in themselves and others.

In this way, control becomes a tool to strengthen relationships and foster an environment of collaboration and mutual growth.

Control as healthy empowerment

Eights may fear being vulnerable and being exposed to situations that make them feel weak or helpless. However, it is important for them to recognize this impulse and be aware of how it can affect their relationships and emotional well-being.

To transform control into healthy empowerment, they need to identify the underlying reasons for their need for control, which may be related to past experiences of trauma or vulnerability;

understanding these roots will help them address them more effectively.

Once they understand the roots of their need for control, it is important that they work on trusting themselves and others. This involves developing greater confidence in their own skills and abilities, as well as trusting in the ability of others to take responsibility and make decisions.

Part of transforming control into healthy empowerment involves accepting and acknowledging that it is natural to feel vulnerable in certain situations, as well as allowing themselves to express and process these emotions, which gives them greater authenticity and connection with others.

In the workplace, a leader eight can transform his or her need for control by assigning tasks to his or her team and allowing them to take responsibility; in a couple's relationship, he or she can work on balancing control by practicing openness and communication.

In situations of stress or conflict, an eight can transform their impulse to control by learning to manage anger constructively. Instead of imposing their will or dominating the situation, they can practice conflict resolution techniques such as open dialogue, empathy and finding mutually beneficial solutions.

In your personal growth, you can look for activities that challenge you to let go of control and explore your more vulnerable side. This could include participating in therapy or support groups, practicing creative activities where you feel less safe, and learning to trust your intuition and others.

Transforming control into healthy empowerment is a significant process for type eight. By recognizing their impulse to control, exploring the underlying roots, cultivating trust, practicing open communication, delegating responsibility, accepting vulnerability, and managing anger constructively, eights can develop a more balanced relationship with control.

In doing so, they open themselves up to more enriching experiences, healthier relationships and a greater sense of personal empowerment.

CHAPTER 11

Personality type 9: Peacemaker

The Peacemaker has a natural tendency to avoid conflict and to maintain peace and harmony in his environment, but this desire leads him to postpone his own needs and desires, losing sight of his priorities.

Type nines often accommodate others to avoid conflict, which can lead them to neglect their own needs. It is important for type nines to recognize this tendency and become aware of how they dilute themselves in favor of others. They can begin by identifying situations in which they feel uncomfortable or resentful about not being able to express themselves or set boundaries.

To find their voice and priorities, type nines must connect with their inner world, taking time for self-reflection. They can ask themselves what they really want, what they are passionate about and what values are important to them. Meditation, personal journaling and therapeutic work can be useful tools for this process.

They often avoid conflict and do not set clear boundaries. To find their voice, it is important that they learn to say "no" when necessary, to stand up for their own needs and desires, and to prioritize themselves without guilt.

To find their voice, they could practice expressing their opinions and desires clearly and assertively, starting by sharing their ideas in meetings or group discussions, expressing their preferences in everyday situations, or participating in activities where they can express themselves creatively. In doing so, they will discover the power of their voice and experience greater authenticity and personal satisfaction.

Type nines often have difficulty identifying their priorities and making firm decisions; they need to learn to discern what is really important to them and make decisions based on their own values and goals. It can be helpful to develop a prioritization system that helps them focus on what is meaningful to them and set clear goals that reflect their true priorities.

For type nines, finding their personal voice and priorities involves overcoming their tendency to avoid conflict and to please others. It requires a process of self-exploration, self-awareness and authenticity. As they connect with their inner voice and establish healthy boundaries, they will feel a greater sense of empowerment and authenticity in their daily lives.

Finding one's own voice and priorities does not imply being selfish or disrespectful to others. Type nines can learn to communicate in an assertive and respectful manner, taking into account the needs of others, but without neglecting their own.

As type nines empower themselves, they will find greater personal satisfaction and a deeper connection with themselves and others.

Type nine personality

The personality of Peacemakers is characterized by their desire to maintain peace and harmony in their environment. They are kind, conciliatory and willing to compromise to avoid conflict; they are understanding and empathetic people, able to see different perspectives and find solutions, can create a calm and welcoming environment is appreciated by others.

However, behind their apparent calm, they face internal challenges that lead them to disconnect from their own needs and desires. In their eagerness to avoid conflict, they tend to suppress their emotions and adapt to the expectations of others, losing sight of their own opinions and priorities. This can lead to loss of identity and the perception that their voice is not heard.

They have a tendency toward passivity and procrastination. They may postpone decisions and actions, avoiding difficult or uncomfortable situations, which leads them to feel stuck and directionless.

To unravel their personality and connect with their true self, type nines must become aware of their own needs and desires, set healthy boundaries, express opinions and make decisions aligned with their personal values and goals.

One practice that can be very helpful to them is self-affirmation, identifying and expressing their own needs clearly and assertively. In addition, taking time for activities such as meditation, yoga or writing helps them to reconnect with themselves, fostering greater self-awareness.

As you connect with your true self, you will experience greater authenticity, purpose and fulfillment in your life.

Avoiding conflict

The conflict avoidance of Peacemakers originates from their desire to preserve tranquility in their lives. Type Nines use different strategies to avoid conflict. However, this attitude can have negative consequences in the long run; let's look at some of them.

- Denying their own needs and desires, disconnecting from their emotions and suppressing their opinions to avoid confrontation.

- Merging with others, adapting to expectations and losing sight of their own identities.
- They procrastinate and postpone situations that could generate conflict. This lack of action can lead them to feel stagnant and directionless in their lives.

Although they avoid conflict, they accumulate resentment and internal frustration, which affects their emotional well-being and relationships.

To overcome conflict avoidance, type nines need to gain awareness of their own needs and desires, set healthy boundaries, express their opinions, and make decisions aligned with their personal values and goals. Practicing assertive communication skills and constructive problem-solving is also helpful.

It is essential to find a balance between keeping the peace and authentically expressing what you feel and want. By addressing conflict in a healthy way, Type Nines strengthen their relationships and build a stronger identity. Self-reflection and self-awareness are important tools in this process.

By becoming aware of their tendency to avoid conflict, they can begin to set healthy boundaries, express their needs and opinions with confidence. This will enable them to transform control and conflict avoidance into open and constructive communication.

Overcoming this tendency will lead to a more fulfilling and authentic life.

Seeking harmony

Type Nines seek harmony in their lives and relationships, avoiding conflict and adapting to the needs of others. They are uncomfortable with challenging situations that could disturb their inner peace, preferring to remain calm and seek unity among people.

Peacemakers seek harmony in a variety of ways, adapt easily to others, sacrifice their own opinions and desires to avoid conflict, avoid expressing their true emotions and thoughts, and tend to postpone or delegate decisions to avoid conflicts of interest.

They also tend to act as conciliators and mediators. They seek to keep the peace and find common ground to avoid confrontations or divisions. Their goal is to create a calm and balanced environment where everyone feels comfortable and accepted.

It is common for them to integrate community groups that work to resolve conflicts or foster cooperation between different social groups. They also seek peaceful environments, such as natural spaces or places of retreat, to find balance both internally and externally.

However, it is important that they recognize the challenges of their constant search for harmony. By avoiding conflict and putting the needs of others above their own, they may lose sight of their own goals and desires. They may feel disconnected from themselves and resentful that they are not receiving the attention and recognition they desire.

To develop a healthier quest for harmony, type nines must learn to connect with their own needs and desires, and express their opinion assertively and respectfully. This involves setting clear boundaries, learning to say "no" when necessary, and dealing with conflict constructively, rather than avoiding it altogether.

By connecting with their own needs and expressing their opinion assertively, type nines can find a more authentic and satisfying harmony in their lives.

Developing your own voice

Peacemakers can lose their unique and authentic voice in their desire to maintain harmony. It is essential that they develop a voice of their own in order to find their true identity and experience greater fulfillment in life.

This requires them to connect with their own needs, desires and opinions, and to express themselves authentically. Overcoming fear of conflict and concern about disturbing the peace will allow them to share their thoughts and feelings, resulting in a sense of empowerment and personal strength.

An important step for type nines to develop a voice of their own is to be self-aware. Dedicating time and space to explore their own thoughts and emotions will allow them to connect with what they really want and need in life.

Meditation, reflective writing or personal therapy can be tools to explore your inner world and discover your authentic voice.

Another crucial aspect is learning to set healthy boundaries. Type Nines often give in to the demands of others and find it difficult to say "no". However, by setting clear boundaries and taking care of themselves, they can protect their time, energy and personal space, which gives them the freedom to express their voice and engage in nurturing activities and relationships.

Assertive communication is also useful for developing a voice of your own, expressing opinions and feelings respectfully and directly, without aggressiveness or passivity. Practicing the expression of their voice in everyday situations, such as family conversations or work meetings, will allow them to defend their ideas and perspectives in a firm but respectful manner.

Participating in creative or artistic activities is another example of how type nines can develop a voice of their own. Exploring talents and expressing creativity through music, painting, writing or other forms of artistic expression gives them a platform to be recognized for their unique contributions.

Developing a voice of their own is essential for type nines. By connecting with their own needs, setting healthy boundaries and practicing assertive communication, they can free themselves from the tendency to avoid conflict and find their true identity, and thus feel greater authenticity, fulfillment and satisfaction in their life.

Conclusion

Towards wisdom and compassion

In the course of our journey through the book "RETURNING TO YOURSELF. Discovering your true self through the Enneagram", we have discovered the path of self-knowledge and personal transformation.

We reflect on how our personalities intertwine with the world around us, understanding that self-knowledge is fundamental to living a full and meaningful life.

Through the Enneagram, we have examined our strengths, weaknesses, motivations and fears, recognizing how they influence our relationships and overall well-being.

By understanding our motivations, behavioral patterns and automatic responses, we learned to make more conscious decisions aligned with our values.

The Enneagram has given us a valuable tool to explore our lights and shadows, integrating all facets of our personality and finding inner harmony.

This system invites us to delve into the complexities of our own minds, confronting those parts of ourselves that we would rather ignore.

Beyond understanding our tendencies and behaviors, the Enneagram takes us to a deeper level of connection with our spiritual essence. It shows us how our experiences and challenges can be opportunities for soul growth and evolution. It encourages us to let go of attachment to our limited identities and allow our true nature to shine through.

In this journey of self-discovery and personal growth, we find the power to transform ourselves and the world around us. We become agents of positive change, building authentic relationships and supporting each other in our growth. We recognize that we are all on a personal journey with our own stories, challenges and needs, cultivating greater understanding, empathy and genuine connection.

As we tap into our own wisdom and compassion, we can also become a beacon of light to those around us. Sharing our experiences, knowledge and understanding of the Enneagram contributes to the well-being of the community at large.

We awaken to our true nature, living from a place of love, compassion and wholeness. The Enneagram provides us with a valuable guide to explore our inner self, discover our true identity and embrace wisdom and compassion in our lives.

"RETURN TO YOURSELF. Discovering your true self through the Enneagram" invites us to fully embrace our capacity to be wise and compassionate beings. Within each of us is a spark of divinity waiting to be recognized and nurtured.

Through self-knowledge and constant practice, we awaken to our true nature and live an authentic and meaningful life.

On this path to wisdom and compassion, we find the possibility of being the wise and compassionate person we wish to be.

BONUS 1

Visualization and personal transformation

Visualization can be an effective way to explore and delve deeper within ourselves. It is a powerful tool that allows us to access our imagination and create vivid and meaningful mental images.

Through visualization, we can connect with our deepest goals, dreams and desires, and use this powerful tool to enhance our self-knowledge and personal growth.

In this bonus, we will learn some visualization exercises that will help us transform our lives in a positive and meaningful way.

Let's look at some visualization exercises that can help us enhance our self-knowledge:

The hall of mirrors: Imagine you walk into a room full of mirrors. Each one reflects a different facet of your personality, your strengths, your weaknesses, your dreams and your fears. Look closely at each reflection and reflect on what it reveals about you. Use this visualization to gain a deeper understanding of who you are.

The inner garden: Close your eyes and imagine that you are walking through a beautiful garden. Each element of the garden represents an aspect of your life: the flowers symbolize your relationships, the trees represent your personal growth, and the water reflects your inner tranquility. Notice how each element looks and how they interact with each other. Reflect on what you would like to change, improve or cultivate in your inner garden. Use this visualization to explore your desires and goals in different areas of your life.

Our imagination has a powerful impact on our perception and our ability to create positive change in our lives. Let's use imagination as a tool for positive change.

Travel to the future: Close your eyes and imagine that you are in a distant future, where you have achieved all your goals and feel fully realized. Observe your life in this future and visualize all the details: how you feel, what you have achieved, how you relate to others, etc. Use this visualization to connect with your vision of success and to set clear and motivating goals in the present.

Transformation of limiting beliefs: Identify a belief that is holding you back from moving toward your goals. Close your eyes and imagine holding that belief in your hands. Visualize transforming that belief into something positive and empowering. Imagine the belief becoming a seed that you plant in the fertile soil of your mind, and enjoy how it grows into a new belief that strengthens you and propels you toward success.

Remember that visualization is a personal and unique practice for each person. You can adapt the visualization exercises to your own needs and preferences. Find a quiet place, close your eyes, breathe deeply and immerse yourself in the imaginative experience.

By using these powerful visualizations, you will develop a deeper connection with yourself, discovering new possibilities and potentialities in your life.

Visualization not only helps you focus on your goals and dreams, but also provides you with an effective tool to overcome obstacles, strengthen your confidence and awaken your creativity.

As you immerse yourself in your imagination, you open yourself to new perspectives and possibilities, creating a solid foundation for growth and positive change in your life. In this way, you can move toward manifesting your true self and living a full and meaningful life.

Visualizations are a valuable tool for personal transformation, allowing you to enhance your self-knowledge, explore your desires and goals, and transform limiting beliefs into empowering ones.

BONUS 2

Affirmations for self-transformation

Affirmations are positive statements that help us to reprogram our minds and promote positive change in our lives. In the context of the Enneagram, we can use specific affirmations based on each personality type to promote self-transformation and personal growth.

Next, let's see which affirmations are effective in helping each personality type on a daily basis:

Personality Type 1 - The Perfectionist

- I am enough as I am. I allow myself to make mistakes and learn from them.
- I recognize that progress is more important than perfection. I allow myself to grow and evolve instead of seeking absolute excellence.
- I appreciate my accomplishments and recognize that success is not determined solely by the end results, but by the effort and dedication I put into each task.

Personality Type 2 - The Helper

- I value my own well-being and set healthy boundaries. I allow myself to be supported and cared for.
- I learn to say "no" when necessary and set healthy boundaries to maintain my emotional and physical well-being.
- I recognize that taking care of myself allows me to be in a better position to help others in a more effective and sustainable way.

Personality Type 3 - The Achiever

- My value does not depend on my external achievements. My authenticity is my greatest strength.
- My worth is not only linked to my external achievements, but to my authenticity and the quality of my personal relationships.
- I appreciate the moments of rest and enjoyment, recognizing that true happiness depends not only on achieving goals, but also on enjoying the journey.

Personality Type 4 - The Individualist

- I celebrate my uniqueness and accept myself in all my facets. My creativity illuminates my path.
- I explore and embrace my inner diversity. Each part of me has its purpose and contributes to my uniqueness and personal growth.
- I appreciate the power of my creativity and allow it to guide my choices, bringing new perspectives and opportunities into my life.

Personality Type 5 - The Researcher

- I trust my inner wisdom and share my knowledge with others. I am part of the whole.
- I trust my intuition and inner wisdom when making decisions and seeking knowledge. My unique perspective enriches my environment and benefits others.
- I generously share my knowledge and experiences, knowing that in doing so, I contribute to the growth and development of those around me.

Personality Type 6 - The Loyal

- I trust myself and the process of life. I am brave and capable of facing any challenge.
- I am confident in myself and in my ability to face challenges. I am constantly growing and developing, and I have the courage to overcome any obstacle that comes my way.
- I cultivate relationships based on loyalty and mutual trust, creating a supportive and collaborative environment in my life.

Personality Type 7 - The Enthusiast

- I find fulfillment in the present and appreciate the blessings of each moment. Joy is within me.
- I find joy and fulfillment in every present moment, appreciating the little things that bring me happiness and gratitude.
- I cultivate a mindset of abundance and optimism, recognizing that joy and happiness are internal states that I can nurture and experience at any time.

Personality Type 8 - The Protector

- I am strong and powerful, I allow myself to be vulnerable and show compassion to others.
- I recognize my personal strength and power, and also allow myself to show vulnerability and compassion to others.
- I use my strength and protection to care for and support those I care about, creating a safe and loving environment around me.

Personality Type 9 - Peacemaker

- I assert myself and express my needs clearly and assertively. My voice is important and valued.
- I assert and express my needs and desires in a clear and respectful manner, knowing that my voice and opinions are important and valued.
- I seek harmony and peaceful conflict resolution, creating a space where everyone feels heard and understood.

For the good use of these and other positive affirmations, it is recommended:

Be aware of your thoughts: Observe your thoughts and detect negative or limiting patterns.

Identify the beliefs you want to change and replace them with positive affirmations.

Choose powerful affirmations: Create affirmations that resonate with you and are relevant to your personal growth. They should be positive, in the present tense and formulated in the first person.

Repeat and reinforce: Repeat your affirmations daily, preferably in moments of peace, when waking up or before going to sleep. Reinforce their effectiveness by visualizing yourself living the reality you desire while reciting them.

Reinforce your affirmations with consistent actions: Affirmations are most effective when they are accompanied by consistent actions. Align your actions and behaviors with the beliefs and attitudes you wish to manifest in your life.

By using affirmations based on each personality type of the Enneagram, you can direct your focus to the specific aspects you wish to strengthen and transform in your life.

Remember that affirmations are not a magical solution but a tool to help you reprogram your mind and create positive change in your life.

Using effective affirmations requires commitment and consistent practice. As you practice and commit to affirmations, you will gradually begin to cultivate a more positive, confident and empowered mindset.

Change takes time and effort. Be patient with yourself and maintain an attitude of openness and receptivity. Do not expect instant results, but practice consistently and trust the process.

By adopting positive and realistic affirmations, you can reprogram your mind and begin to align your thoughts, beliefs and actions with your true potential.

Don't be discouraged if at first you don't feel an immediate change, consistent practice and perseverance are key to lasting results. Over time, affirmations can help you change your negative thought patterns, strengthen your self-confidence and enable you to achieve your goals and aspirations.

Adapt affirmations to your own language and way of thinking. Choose words and phrases that generate a sense of connection and empowerment. Affirmations must be realistic and believable to you, as your mind needs to accept them as true to be effective.

As you practice affirmations consistently and integrate them into your daily life, you will begin to notice positive changes in the way you think, feel and act. For example, if you affirm that you are a healthy person, support that affirmation with healthy food choices and regular exercise.

Powerful affirmations can be an invaluable tool for self-transformation and personal growth. By combining effective affirmations with clear visualizations and consistent actions, you can cultivate a positive mindset and build a life more aligned with your true self.

BONUS 3

Cultivating Emotional Resilience

Emotional resilience is an essential ability to face life's challenges and adversities with strength and adaptability. It allows us to recover from difficulties and maintain a positive attitude.

Emotional resilience is essential to our emotional and mental well-being, helping us to cope with stressful situations, overcome failures and maintain a positive mindset. By cultivating it, we develop the ability to manage our emotions in a healthy way and build a solid foundation for personal growth.

There are several aspects that emotional resilience can strengthen in our personality. For example:

Adaptation to change: Allows us to adapt to life's changes and transitions more effectively. It helps us to accept and overcome obstacles, finding new opportunities in the midst of adversity.

Stress management: Helps us to manage stress more efficiently. It allows us to identify our emotional responses to stressful situations and take measures to reduce the negative impact of stress on our health and well-being.

Self-confidence: Strengthens our self-confidence. It helps us believe in our abilities to overcome challenges and gives us the courage to face difficult situations.

There are several practices that can help you strengthen your emotional resilience. Here are some recommended exercises and techniques:

Emotional self-awareness: Take the time to explore and understand your own emotions. Practice mindfulness and introspection to recognize your emotional patterns and how they affect you. This will allow you to develop a greater awareness of yourself and your emotional responses.

Building a support network: Cultivate strong and supportive relationships with family, friends and members of your community. Share your feelings and experiences with people you trust, as this can give you the emotional support you need during difficult times.

Seek social support: Seek support from people close to you, such as friends, family or support groups. Sharing your experiences and emotions with others can help you gain different perspectives and feel understood. Participate in social activities that provide positive connections and allow you to feel part of a community.

Practice self-compassion: Learn to treat yourself with kindness and understanding when you face challenges or make mistakes. Recognize that we all make mistakes and that personal growth involves learning from them. Instead of judging yourself harshly, practice self-compassion and give yourself permission to be human.

Maintain a learning attitude: Cultivate a mindset that is open and receptive to continuous learning. Consider every experience as an opportunity to grow and learn more about yourself. Be curious and willing to explore new perspectives and approaches in life.

Acceptance and adaptation: Learn to accept circumstances that you cannot change and focus on adapting to them. Recognize that change is an inevitable part of life and look for new ways to deal with challenges.

Problem-solving practice: Develops effective problem-solving skills. Break challenges into smaller, more manageable steps and look for creative solutions. This will help you face obstacles with a proactive mindset.

Self-care: Prioritize your physical and mental well-being. Spending time on activities that bring you joy, rest and rejuvenation is critical to cultivating emotional resilience. Set healthy boundaries in your life and learn to say "no" when necessary. Self-care also involves eating a balanced diet, getting enough rest and maintaining a proper sleep routine.

Develop coping skills: Learn healthy coping techniques to manage stress and negative emotions. This may include regular physical exercise, relaxation techniques such as meditation or deep breathing, and finding activities that help you express your emotions, such as writing in a journal or practicing a hobby.

Cultivate positive thoughts: Practice gratitude and focus on positive aspects of your life. Challenge your negative thoughts and replace them with positive affirmations. Make a list of past accomplishments and personal strengths to remind you of your ability to overcome obstacles and face challenges.

Developing emotional resilience is an ongoing process that requires practice and dedication. By strengthening our ability to manage emotions and adapt to difficult situations, we can face life's challenges with confidence and maintain a positive outlook.

Use these exercises and techniques to build a solid foundation for your emotional well-being and personal growth.

Remember to be kind to yourself during this journey of self-transformation.

BONUS 4

Building Healthy Relationships

Healthy, meaningful relationships are fundamental to our emotional and personal well-being. They provide us with support, companionship and a sense of deep connection. However, building healthy relationships can be challenging, as each individual brings unique experiences and patterns of behavior.

The basis of any healthy relationship is open and honest communication; this implies:

- Learn to express our feelings, thoughts and needs in a clear and respectful manner.
- Actively listen to your partner, friend or family member, showing genuine interest and empathy.
- Establishing clear boundaries in relationships is essential to ensure mutual respect and emotional balance.
- Learn to say "no" when necessary and to set limits in uncomfortable situations.

Trust is a fundamental pillar of healthy relationships. To build it, it is important:

- Be authentic.
- Fulfill promises and commitments.
- Avoid manipulation, dishonesty and deception.
- Practice empathy and understanding by putting yourself in the other person's shoes and validating their emotions and perspectives.
- Identify and address toxic patterns, abusive behaviors or disrespect in relationships.

Overcoming toxic patterns requires personal work and a commitment to each other. You can seek professional support or consider therapy to work on healing and change.

It is important to remember that each relationship is unique and requires constant attention. By developing a greater awareness of yourself and your relationship patterns, you will be able to nurture and strengthen your connections with others.

Remember that healthy relationships also involve taking care of yourself. Set boundaries and make time for physical and mental self-care.

By building healthy relationships, you will be cultivating an environment of support, trust and mutual growth. Through mindfulness and commitment, you can create lasting, meaningful relationships that propel you toward a fuller, more satisfying life.

Thank you for your interest in reading my work

I hope you have found this book interesting and that by reading my experiences, you have gained ideas and inspiration to help you on your own path to self-improvement, mental health and happiness.

I invite you to continue on the path of self-help.

Keep reading the entire collection of self-help books I have created for you, keep getting ideas and inspiration for self-improvement, mental health and happiness.

Your help means a lot

If you liked this book, one of the best things you could do for me would be to leave a review on the website where you bought it. It won't take you long, but it would be great if you could spare those minutes for me.

If you give my work a high rating, more people will see it and, in turn, it will improve their lives, health and happiness.

May your journey be filled with peace and abundance,

Simone Keys

Printed in Great Britain
by Amazon

33831891R00121